BERLITZ®

W9-DJM-372

CANCÚN and COZUMEL

- A ✔ in the text denotes a highly recommended sight
- A complete A–Z of practical information starts on p. 109
- Extensive mapping throughout: on cover flaps and in text

Berlitz Trademark Reg. US Patent Office and other countries. Marca Registrada.

Printed in Switzerland by Weber SA, Bienne.

2nd edition (1994/5)

Although we make every effort to ensure the accuracy of the information in this guide, changes do occur. If you have any new information, suggestions or corrections to contribute, we would like to hear from you. Please write to Berlitz Publishing at the above address.

Text:	Neil Wilson
Editor:	Jane Middleton
Photography:	Neil Wilson
Cartography:	HardLines
Layout:	Visual Image
Thanks to:	The Mexican Government Tourism Office for their valuable assistance in the preparation of this guide.

CONTENTS

Cancún, Cozumel and the Yucatán

For centuries the Yucatán peninsula has drawn adventurers to it: Spanish conquistadors in pursuit of gold and glory, and buccaneers seeking harbours safe from prying eyes; archaeologists hacking through the jungle in search of ruined cities; divers plumbing the depths of the crystal Caribbean in the hunt for sunken treasure. The advent of air travel and modern highways has made the area much less remote, but for today's traveller there is still plenty of adventure around.

Look at a map of the Caribbean, and you will see the Yucatán peninsula sticking into the Gulf of Mexico like a great thumb ready to pinch Cuba's tail against the slender finger of Florida. Near the tip of the thumb lies Cancún, Mexico's most popular holiday destination, and its neighbouring island resort, Cozumel.

When the American adventurer John Lloyd Stephens sailed along the remote eastern coast of the Yucatán peninsula in 1842 in search of ruined Mayan cities, he stopped briefly on 'the island of Kancune, a barren strip of land, with sand hills and stone buildings visible upon it'. After a swim, and a stroll along the magnificent beach at Punta Nizuc, his party set sail for Cozumel, leaving their footprints to be washed away by the warm Caribbean waves. And for more than a century afterwards the island of Cancún remained a deserted strip of sand dunes and scrub, its only buildings the few small Mayan ruins, its only inhabitants a handful of itinerant Mayan fishermen.

Until very recently, the sands of Cancún remained untrodden except by wandering native Mayan fishermen and a few adventurous travellers. Then in 1967 the Mexican government began investigating the potential for tourism of various sites, encouraged by the earning power of established resorts like Acapulco. With clear warm waters, beautiful beaches and coral reefs, it **5**

*M*ayan ruins and tropical blooms characterize the country-side around Cancún.

is hardly surprising that the Isla de Cancún made it on to the shortlist. As the now-famous story goes, the vital statistics for all the different locations were fed into a computer and the machine printed out the name 'Cancún' top of the list.

Cancún is an island shaped like a '7', only 400 yds (365 m) wide, but over 12 miles (19 km) long – 12 miles of beautiful, blindingly white, coral-sand beaches; on one side the crystal clear, turquoise waters of the Caribbean, on the other the sheltered Nichupté Lagoon, perfect for sailing and wind-surfing. It offers an average of 243 sun-drenched days each year, with temperatures that rarely dip below the 80s, easy access to the idyllic islands of Isla Mujeres and Cozumel, spectacular coral reefs and magnificent Mayan ruins; all within a few hours' flying time

easy to reach. Nearly everyone speaks some English, and US dollars are readily accepted.

But what makes Cancún special is its incomparable setting. The Yucatán landscape is a heady tropical cocktail of deep green jungle and azure ocean, sprinkled with a colourful garnish of exotic wildlife. In the jungle, spider monkeys and bright-billed toucans flit beneath the trees, while bright-winged butterflies and emerald lizards flutter and skitter among the dappled shadows of the forest floor. Along the coast, spiky-backed iguanas bask on jagged rocks like miniature dinosaurs, pelicans patrol the waves in search of good fishing and flamingos flock in their thousands to favoured lagoons. Coconut groves fringe endless strands of ivory sand, where lugubrious turtles lumber ashore in the dead of night in summer to lay their eggs.

of many major American cities – the perfect location.

Development of Cancún began in 1970. The plan was simpe – a line of luxury hotels along the island, which was to be joined to the mainland at each end by a bridge. At the north end, a city to house the people who would work in the hotels, restaurants and other businesses; at the south end an international airport. Just over 20 years later Cancún is a mega-resort, a sun-drenched paradise to the two million tourists who flock here each year. It's a user-friendly resort – top-quality accommodation, beaches on your doorstep, excellent modern facilities,

Look again at the map and you will see that there are no rivers in the Yucatán. The peninsula underlying the jungle is a flat, low-lying shelf of limestone, pock-marked with count- **7**

Goats seek out the shade beneath the palms at Tulum, while
8 (above right) an iguana soaks up the noon-day sun.

ancient and modern, simple and sophisticated. Within a few hours' drive of the concrete and glass towers of the Hotel Zone you will find the pyramids and temples of ruined Mayan cities, half-hidden in the encroaching jungle. You can shop till you drop in the designer boutiques of Cancún's glittering shopping malls, and the next day bargain in the market for a hand-woven hammock. You can travel to the offshore islands on board an air-cushioned catamaran, or head for a beach picnic on a traditional wooden fishing boat.

less caverns and sink-holes, which soaks up the rain like a sponge. The lack of rivers means that no silt is carried into the sea, leaving the warm waters of the Mexican Caribbean sparklingly clear, ideal for the growth of coral reefs. The reefs around Cozumel are some of the most spectacular in the world, and draw thousands of divers each year to marvel at the magnificent marine life or search for the wrecks of sunken Spanish galleons.

This splendid setting also offers a curious juxtaposition of

You will soon notice that the inhabitants of Cancún, rather like the city, are young, bright and appealing. Most have moved to Cancún from other parts of Mexico to make money, learn English, and enjoy the climate – on weekends the public beaches are jammed with locals as well as visitors. In contrast, the surrounding country is peopled by the quiet, dignified Maya Indians, whose ancestors worked the land for thousands of years and saw the rise and fall of a mighty civilization. **9**

Spanish colonial towns with fortress churches, villages of thatched huts and rough fields of corn, and the quiet dignified faces of the Maya; underground caverns the size of cathedrals, the walls carved with ancient graffiti; limpid lagoons alive with bird life; jungle-fringed cenotes of cool, clear water, inviting you to swim; rocky inlets and desert islands; colourful coral reefs and deep ocean waters teeming with marlin and barracuda.

All this and more is out there, beyond the Cancún city limits, just waiting for you to explore. So take a break from the sun-worshipping, jump into the jeep, and seek out a little adventure.

A water-skier manages to snatch a final run as the sun sets beyond idyllic, sheltered Nichupte Lagoon.

A Brief History

There are few places in the world where the past feels as close as it does in the Yucatán. The thatched huts which appear in 1000-year-old carvings at Uxmal can be seen today in roadside villages. The stone *metates*, or grinding dishes, which grace many a kitchen in town or village, are identical to those left as offerings to the rain gods in centuries past. Away from the cities the people still speak the Mayan tongue, and their religious beliefs still bear the imprint of the ancient rituals of the Maya. And perhaps most striking of all, the distinctive hooked nose and sloping foreheads of the ancient Maya, whose stony profiles look down on the visitor from the carved walls of their ruined cities, are reflected in the features of the local people.

The Maya

Although their ruined cities stand witness to their many achievements, little is known for certain about the Mayan people themselves. Written records are extremely rare, and it is only very recently that scholars have been able to decipher Mayan hieroglyphics. But a patchy history has been pieced together using dates

How did Yucatán get its Name?

One story claims that the captain of one of the first Spanish ships to reach the peninsula went ashore and was met by a delegation of Indians. The captain asked the chief (in Spanish of course) 'What land is this?', and the Indian's answer was 'Ci u than', which meant 'I do not understand your words' in the native language. The captain heard this as 'Yucatan', and so the name stuck. Another theory says that the name comes from the local Yucca plant, plus 'tal' or 'thale', which means the heap of earth in which the plant grows.

Magnificent architecture is testament to the achievements of Mayan civilization.

carved on *stelae* (inscribed stone pillars) and radiocarbon dating of wooden items.

These people's ancestors arrived in Central America many thousands of years ago, as small bands of Asiatic hunters migrated across the Bering Straits land bridge and gradually spread southwards through the Americas. Between 2000 BC and AD 250 the group that came to be known as the Maya settled in an area which stretched from the Pacific coast

corn came to symbolize life for the Maya – in their myths on creation, mankind was formed from lumps of maize dough. Elaborate rituals grew up around the preparation of the *milpas* (corn-fields), and the planting and harvesting of the crop. The importance of the rains is reflected in the worship of Chaac (the Mayan rain god) whose long-nosed mask scowls down from the walls of so many Mayan buildings.

In the succeeding centuries, this area witnessed the flowering of classic Maya civilization, with its magnificent pyramids, temples and palaces decorated with wall paintings and carved low-reliefs, a written language of hieroglyphics, a complex counting system based on the number 20, and an elaborate calendar that is more accurate even than our own (see also p.58). Mayan astronomers tracked the movements of the heavenly bodies, predicting eclipses and marking the times for the planting of the new corn.

to the northern Yucatán, taking in modern-day Guatemala and Belize, the western parts of El Salvador and Honduras, and the Mexican states of Campeche, Yucatán, Quintana Roo and part of Tabasco.

They developed a primitive agriculture, based mainly on the cultivation of corn, beans, chilli peppers and squash (a pumpkin-like vegetable) in burned clearings in the jungle, whose success depended on the coming of the annual rains. In fact,

But there was a dark side to this sophisticated society. The gods demanded more offerings **13** than food and incense – they wanted human lives. A cult of human sacrifice grew, and the murals and reliefs of the Maya tell a gory tale of beheadings and tearing out of human hearts to appease the lords of the underworld. Archaeologists dredging the Sacred Cenote of Chichén Itzá have recovered dozens of human skeletons, the remains of victims sacrificed to the rain god.

Mayan civilization in the northern Yucatán reached its peak around AD 900-1200. For reasons still unknown – perhaps civil war, drought or disease – the great cities were abandoned. By the time the Spaniards arrived in the early 16th century the jungle was reclaiming the pyramids and plazas; the richly painted murals of warriors and Mayan lords, animals and gods were crumbling and dissolving in the warm rain.

In the Wake of Cortés

The first recorded Europeans to arrive in the Yucatán, in 1511, were doubly unfortunate: a group of Spanish sailors sur-vived a shipwreck on the coast of what is now Quintana Roo, only to be sacrificed by the Mayan natives. However, two were allowed to live as slaves and one, Gonzalo Guerrero, went native and married the chief's daughter. Their children were the first *mestizos* – the people of mixed Indian and Spanish blood who now make up 55 per cent of the Mexican population.

In 1517, an expedition led by Francisco Hernandez de Cordobá landed on the west coast of the Yucatán, near Campeche, but were beaten back by a hail of arrows from the hostile natives. However, the following year an ambitious young captain, Juan de Grijalva, discovered the island of Cozumel and skirted the coast of the peninsula, hearing tales from the Indians of the great civilization of the Aztecs.

Grijalva's stories focused Spanish attention on central Mexico, and in 1519 Hernan Cortés landed in Veracruz, to start an expedition that would end in the conquest of Moctezuma and the Aztec Empire.

Colonial splendour – the Plaza Principal in Mérida.

It was left to Don Francisco de Montejo, 'a gentleman of Seville', following in the great conquistador's wake, to take possession of the Yucatán in the name of the Spanish king.

Arriving on the coast in 1527, Montejo's forces were hindered by the dense jungle and withering climate, and were met by fierce resistance from the natives. To make matters worse, news of the great riches discovered in Peru led many of his men to desert. The campaign went so badly that by 1535 the Spaniards had been completely driven out of the Yucatán.

In 1537 another expeditionary force, under the command of Montejo el Mozo (the Younger), Don Francisco's son, set out to plant the Spanish standard on Yucatán soil. At first ill fortune dogged them, and the dwindling force was besieged in Champoton on the west coast for two miserable years. With reinforcements, the Spaniards managed to push north to Campeche, where they established their beach head. From there a band of only 57 men, led by Montejo el Mozo's cousin (yet another Don Francisco), marched inland to take the Mayan town of T'Ho. The Indians gathered their forces for one last great battle, and thou- **15** sands of them fell upon the Spanish camp, now defended by 200 men. The horses and superior weaponry of the Spaniards gave them the edge, and they slaughtered hundreds of Indian warriors. After the battle, local chiefs made peace with the invaders and, on 6 January 1542, the Montejos founded the Spanish city of Mérida on the site of T'Ho.

The Caste War

Under Spanish rule, lands were taken from the Maya and turned over to tobacco and sugarcane plantations, and the once-proud Indians were reduced to farm labourers. Franciscan friars such as the 16th-century Bishop Diego de Landa, spread the Christian faith throughout the peninsula, though they were met with some resistance – any similarity between the early Yucatán churches and military fortresses is not accidental. The Maya accepted the new faith, but combined it with elements of their old beliefs.

Furthermore, the isolation of Yucatán from the rest of Mexico led to the development of a strong independent streak. Following Mexico's declaration of independence from Spain in 1821, the Yucatán threatened to declare independence from Mexico. The political sniping was overshadowed in 1847, however, when the Maya decided that after three centuries of colonial oppression enough was enough. In a savage uprising known as the Caste War, the Mayan rebels massacred white settlers and took control of nearly two-thirds of the peninsula, and by 1850 they had driven the Mexicans back to their strongholds in Mérida and Campeche.

However, in an amazing turnaround, the Maya's ancient beliefs became their undoing. Just when the Mexicans were on the point of surrender, the rains came early and the Indians, obedient to their gods, dropped their weapons and returned to their *milpas* to plant the sacred corn. The settlers called in reinforcements and wreaked a terrible revenge on the natives. But one group of rebels, known as the Chan

Santa Cruz, held out in the jungles of Quintana Roo, harrying the Mexicans and making the east coast of the Yucatán a dangerous no-go area until well into the 20th century.

The Henequen Boom

In the late 19th century, the *hacienda* owners of the northern Yucatán grew rich on the proceeds from their henequen plantations. The ropes and twines manufactured from the fibres of the henequen plant (*sisal*) were in great demand, and Yucatán was the principal producer.

The money was spent on grand mansions along Mérida's Paseo de Montejo, packed with luxuries, while the Indians worked the plantations for a pittance. In the east, some scraped a living by tapping the sap of the zapote tree (*chicle*), and selling it to American manufacturers of chewing-gum. The henequen bubble burst with increasing competition from Cuban growers, and the advent of synthetic fibres in the 1930s.

Henequen

The henequen plant is a member of the *agave* family (other species of agave are used in the production of tequila). Its spiky, grey-green leaves have been used as a source of fibre since pre-Hispanic times. Plantation owners made their fortunes growing and exporting henequen fibre in the 18th and 19th centuries, flaunting their wealth in the grandiose mansions they built along the Paseo Montejo in Mérida. The fibre was made into twine and rope used in agriculture and shipping, and was used locally to make bags, hammocks and shoe soles. In the USA and Europe it was called *sisal*, after the port of Sisal on the north coast of the Yucatán, whence the bales of henequen were exported.

Meanwhile, under the presidency of Porfirio Diaz, Quintana Roo, named after Andreas Quintana Roo, a writer and leader active in the independence movement between 1810 and 1821, was declared a territory of Mexico in 1902. Government troops clamped down harshly on rebellious Indians, but they continued to resist, and it was not until 1935 that a peace treaty was finally negotiated. The overthrow of Porfirio

Diaz and the new constitution of 1917 led to reform, including a bill of rights for Mexican workers, under which many haciendas were broken up and returned to the people. But the Yucatán remained a backwater

Sun-worshippers flock to the beautiful beaches of Cancún to indulge in their calm turquoise waters and velvet sands.

on the fringe of Mexico, largely forgotten and ignored. No overland route existed from Mérida to the rest of Mexico until 1949, when the first railway arrived. Before then, all commercial travel to and from the peninsula was by sea, and it was faster and easier to travel to Cuba or the USA than to Mexico City.

Mexico's Mega-resort

Despite its considerable oil reserves and mineral wealth, the economy of modern Mexico has been crippled by debt, booming population growth and grinding poverty. In an effort to bring more hard currency into the country the government decided to promote tourism. A three-year study of various sites was conducted by a consortium of government and private interests, and the deserted island of Cancún came up trumps: not only was it a beautiful spot, but also its use would revive the flagging economy of the Yucatán and finally bring Quintana Roo into the fold – the territory was eventually granted statehood in 1974.

Cancún is now Mexico's most popular holiday destination, pulling in two million tourists each year. Business booms. New roads have appeared, water purification plants have been built, televisions and refrigerators are now the norm in villages that didn't even have electricity 15 years ago.

The question now is, can the development be controlled? What was a deserted coastline two decades ago is now a bustling riviera. Coral reefs are being damaged by careless divers. Lagoons that once teemed with tropical fish are being polluted by the sun-tan lotion and rubbish left in the water by hordes of tourists. The beaches where sea turtles once laid their eggs are being taken over by sun-loungers and volleyball nets. The crocodiles and manatees that once haunted the coastal waters are now endangered species. The next big struggle in the history of the Yucatán will be one that is being faced all over the world – the battle between the conflicting demands of development and conservation.

Where to go

Cancún

Pop. 250,000

Cancún is divided into two parts, Cancún City (*Ciudad Cancún*) and the Hotel Zone (*Zona Hotelera*). Commuting between the two is fast and easy, with buses coming along every few minutes and taxis continuously touting for business.

Cancún City is the bustling new town built on the mainland to house the many people who work in Cancún's hotels, restaurants and services. Life in downtown Cancún (*el centro*) revolves around the traffic-crammed Avenida Tulum, the broad main road lined with restaurants, shops, supermarkets and travel agencies. A number of shopping plazas lead off the pavements, including the open-air **Ki-Huic** handicrafts market – a good cruising ground for souvenir hunters. A number of hotels may also be found here, mostly in the moderate to budget price range.

Running parallel to Tulum, a block to the west, is Avenida Yaxchilán, where you can indulge in shopping and eating at slightly lower prices. Between the two lies the **Parque de las Palapas**, an open square that plays host to markets and open-air weekend concerts, where locals and tourists can party together. Halfway along Yaxchilán, Avenida Sunyaxchen leads to Cancún's main post office (*correo*).

At the north end of Tulum, near the Tourist Information Office, is the **City Hall** (*Ayuntamiento Benito Juárez*), which organizes evenings of traditional Mexican and Caribbean music on the esplanade in front of the hall (Fridays and Saturdays at 9 p.m.). If you are lucky enough to be here during Carnival time (the week preceding Shrove Tuesday), you can join the crowds following the procession of floats to the crowning of the Carnival Queen.

If your taste in entertainment runs to something more bloodthirsty, you can share in part of Mexico's Spanish heritage at the Plaza de Toros – the

Bullring, on Avenida Bonampak. Bullfights are staged here each Wednesday at 3.30 p.m.

Avenida Tulum continues north to Avenida Lopez Portillo, where you turn right for Puerto Juárez and the ferry to Isla Mujeres, or left for the road to Chichén Itzá and Mérida. Heading south, Avenida Tulum becomes the main road along the coast towards the airport and on to Tulum.

The **Hotel Zone** stretches along a narrow 14-mile (23 km) dog-leg of dazzling white beach, backed by the limpid waters of Laguna Nichupté. A single boulevard, Paseo Kukulcán, winds the full length of the Hotel Zone from the *glorieta* (roundabout) at the edge of downtown, to Club Med at Punta Nizuc, and continues towards the airport. Kilometre posts mark the distances from downtown; memorize which one is nearest your hotel and you will find it easier to remember where to get off the bus.

The beaches of Cancún are justly famous. The blindingly white sand is a product of coral, shell and limestone, pounded

and sifted by the Caribbean surf, perfectly set off by the turquoise and ultramarine of the sea. The sand reflects sunlight so well that it rarely gets hot enough to be uncomfortable under bare feet. But beware: the reflected light can also increase the likelihood of sunburn. It has been said many times, but it's worth repeating – sunburn is easier to prevent than cure, so don't let it ruin your holiday.

The north-facing beaches between downtown and Punta Cancún are wide and sheltered, and safest for swimming: the long, east-facing strand from Punta Cancún to Punta Nizuc gets bigger waves and some of the beaches there can develop a dangerous undertow.

Most hotels have lifeguards who patrol the beach, and fly coloured flags to warn of dangerous sea conditions. A red or black flag means danger, keep out of the water; yellow means

Isla Mujeres shimmers on the horizon above the lovely Playa Linda beach.

that competent swimmers can bathe with caution; green or blue means conditions are safe for all.

Although the beach-front hotels provide lifeguards, sun-loungers, parasols, showers, snack-bars and other facilities for the use of their guests, the beaches are not private. All beaches in Mexico are federal property and are open to the general public, so even if you are staying in one of the hotels downtown you can wander freely along any stretch of sand in Cancún. There are several public access points with car-parking, such as at Playa Tortugas, Playa Caracol and Playa Chac Mool, from where you can walk along the sand to wherever you fancy.

Heading along Paseo Kukulcán, at the 4 km marker you will reach the bridge joining Isla Cancún to the mainland. The Canal Nichupté carries a steady stream of traffic commuting between the lagoon and the open sea. To the left of the bridge is the **Playa Linda Marine Terminal**, from which boats depart for day trips to Isla **23**

The ruins of the former watchtower, Yamil Lu'um, grace the highest point of Isla Cancún.

Mujeres, Contoy and Cozumel. This is also the place to catch a glass-bottomed boat for a close encounter with the coral reefs in the Bahía de Mujeres, the sheltered bay lying between the northern beaches and Isla Mujeres. The bay is a perfect spot for windsurfing and sailing; boards and boats may be hired on the beach at Playa Linda, across the canal from the quay. The headquarters of the Mexican National Windsurfing Association is just along the road, and the National Windsurfing Tournament is held here each July.

Between the 6 and 7 km markers you pass through part of the **Pok-Ta-Pok Golf Course**, which is beautifully landscaped among the palm trees. The course stretches out along a narrow island in the lagoon, and out near the 12th green are some small Mayan ruins. Pok-Ta-Pok is the indigenous name for the ancient Mayan ball game in which the losers' heads were chopped off – hopefully all that'll get sliced here is your opponent's drive!

Where the island 'turns the corner' at Punta Cancún is the nearest the Hotel Zone comes to having a town centre. A cluster of shopping malls, restaurants, bars and nightclubs lines the Paseo here, and draws big crowds at lunchtime and in the evenings. **Plaza Caracol** is one of the biggest shopping centres, and inside the main entrance you can find the Cancún Tips desk, an independent tourist information service whose staff are friendly and helpful. Across from the Caracol is the site of the **Convention Centre**. The Centre is being rebuilt and expanded after suffering damage during Hurricane Gilbert in 1988. It is scheduled to reopen in 1995.

Just past km 12, on the left, is the Sheraton Hotel, in the grounds of which is the highest point of land on Isla Cancún, all of 45 ft (14 m) above the sea. This little limestone crag is capped by the Mayan ruins called **Yamil Lu'um**, a small building that may have served as a watchtower or lighthouse in ancient times. The view is magnificent.

Two other big shopping malls are situated nearby: Plaza Flamingo is between km 11 and 12, and the new Plaza Kukulcán is at km 13.

Beachfront development begins to thin out a little as you pass the impressive glass pyramid of the Hotel Meliá Cancún, and the equally impressive, 117 ft (36 m) tall, thatched *palapa* of its neighbour, the Fiesta Americana Condesa.

At km 17 a dirt road on the right leads to the archaeological site of **Ruinas El Rey**. This small Mayan site dates from the late post-classic period (AD 1200-1530), and was probably a ceremonial centre. Early explorers named the site *El Rey* (the king), after they discovered the head of a large statue among the ruins, and human remains in and around the pyramid, which lead them to believe that some important person had been buried there.

There are two groups of buildings. As you enter the site you come to the **Grupo El Rey**, clustered around a plaza. Here, there is a small pyramid, two colonnaded platforms and a low building which contains remnants of painted murals. **25**

The second group of buildings lies to the south, the **Grupo de las Pinturas** (the paintings), which consists of more low platforms and the remains of three small 'palaces'. Unfortunately, the murals which gave the group its name have long since disappeared.

Paseo Kukulcán leads on towards the airport, but the beaches and hotels come to an end at the rocky promontory of **Punta Nizuc**, where Club Med nestles among the palms. There is good snorkelling south west of the point, where the water is sheltered by a rocky reef. You can scramble out to the headland from the shore in front of the Club. Here, iguanas sunbathe on the jagged limestone around the base of the lookout tower. You can look back along the miles of white sand and glittering hotels and imagine what it must have looked like when John Lloyd Stephens put ashore in 1842 and described 'the island of Kancune' as 'a barren strip of land, with sand hills and stone buildings visible upon it'. Times have changed.

Isla Mujeres

Pop. 13,000

When you step ashore on Isla Mujeres, take a moment to cast your eyes skywards above the palm trees to where the frigate birds are flying. You can't mistake the scythe-shaped wings and deeply forked tails of these pirates of the skies, as they patrol the shoreline for unwitting seabirds returning home full of fish. When they spot a likely victim they will harry the hapless bird relentlessly until it disgorges its hard-won cargo of food. The hungry frigate bird will catch the surrendered meal before it hits the water and gulp it down, then return to its vantage point above the palms.

The island was once also the haunt of human pirates: in the 17th and 18th centuries a number of buccaneers had their lairs on Isla Mujeres. The famous American pirate, Jean Lafitte, who terrorized Spanish shipping in the Gulf of Mexico and fought against General Andrew Jackson in the Battle of New Orleans in 1812 in return for a pardon, retired here in the 1820s to escape the attentions of the US government.

Local legend has it that in the early 19th century the Spanish pirate and slave-trader, Fermín Mundaca, fell in love with an island girl, and in a lovelorn attempt to woo her, built a beautiful hacienda just for her. His efforts were in vain, though – the ungrateful wench spurned Mundaca for a younger man and left the old pirate to die heartbroken.

The earliest recorded visitors to the island arrived in 1517. The Spanish explorer Francisco Hernández de Córdoba and his crew landed and discovered a number of small Mayan temples filled with countless sculptures of female figures – probably the fertility goddess Ix Chel – and promptly named the place Isla Mujeres, 'the island of women'.

Although it is a mere 40-minute ferry trip from Cancún, Isla Mujeres feels very different – it is smaller, more laid-back, and low key. The ferry deposits you right in front of the town at the north end of the island.

ISLA MUJERES

N

- Hotel del Prado
- Playa Norte
- Post Office
- Ferry Pier
- Naval Base
- Farito
- Islote Tiburon

CARIBBEAN SEA

Laguna Makax

Salina Grande

BAHÍA DE MUJERES

AV. GUSTAVO RUEDA MEDINA

Playa Lancheros

Site of Hacienda Mundaca

Playa Indios

El Garrafon

Punta Sur

Key:
- Lighthouse
- Places of interest
- Ruins
- Local airport
- Main roads
- Beach

0   1 km
0   ½ mile

Walk straight along the street opposite the pier and you'll run out of land in about three minutes!

On the way you'll pass the small town square where the *isleños* (islanders) gather to gossip, and the local children play basketball. Explore the crafts and souvenir shops in the grid of narrow streets squeezed between the waterfronts, and stop for a meal or a drink at one of the many open-air cafés. Beach bums should turn left from the pier and head straight for **Playa Norte**, the beautiful sandy beach a few blocks north of the square. It's also called Playa Coco – Coconut Beach.

The island is only 5 miles (8 km) long and may be explored easily by bicycle or moped, which you can hire by the hour or day from one of the many agencies in town. The road south leads past the Mexican Naval Base, and along the edge of the Laguna Makax, which was used as a harbour by the pirate fleets of old. The few remains of the hacienda built by the pirate Mundaca lie about 3 miles (5 km) from town, hidden in the undergrowth across the road from Playa Lancheros (there are plans to restore the **Hacienda Mundaca** as a tourist attraction).

Playa Lancheros and its neighbour **Playa Paraiso** are pleasant beaches with *palapa* bars and restaurants, but they are not as good as Playa Norte. There is a small entrance fee for these beaches.

Towards the southern end of the island lies **El Garrafon National Park**, a magnet for day trippers from Cancún. The park's *raison d'être* is a small coral reef which fringes the shore only a few yards out, in water only 10-15 ft (3-4.5 m) deep. The reef's easy access and its population of brightly coloured tropical fish make it a Mecca for first-time snorkellers, who throng the water in their dozens when the cruise boats arrive around lunchtime, so if you want to enjoy the reef in

Snorkellers queue up in order to explore the fascinating coral reef at El Garrafon.

peace, try to arrive as early as possible. Unfortunately, the disturbance caused by hundreds of enthusiastic snorkellers has killed off most of the coral, but there are still plenty of fish to look at. In the shallows inside the reef there are shoals of sergeant-majors (small fish with black-and-yellow striped backs) which are so tame, they will eat bread from your hand.

For a small fee one of the motor boats that hang around the pier at El Garrafon may be hired to take you on a 5-minute ride out to the reefs that lie a little further offshore. Here the water is 15-25 ft (4.5-7.5 m) deep, the coral scenery is far more spectacular, and the marine life more plentiful and varied, with large parrotfish, angelfish, spectacular shoals of grunt, Bermuda chub, and blue tang, and even some small barracuda.

Back at the pier there is a pen containing three or four large nurse sharks. If you're

*R*ugged coastal scenery at Punta Sur on Isla Mujeres.

feeling brave you can swim with them, and perhaps even have your photo taken (so your friends will believe you!). There's no danger, though – nurse sharks are harmless, and so lazy that they will probably take no notice of you.

The park also has a bar and restaurant, showers, changing rooms, lockers, diving shops, snorkelling equipment rental, and pleasant terraces for sun-bathing.

Experienced divers may be tempted to visit the **Cave of the Sleeping Sharks**, made famous on film by Jacques Cousteau. It was once thought that sharks could never rest, and had to swim continuously to keep a flow of water over their gills, or they would die. Cousteau discovered this underwater cavern full of sluggish, somnolent sharks resting on the sea bed. Diving shops at El Garrafón, in town, and in Cancún offer trips to the cave, which lies off the east side of the island.

A few hundred yards beyond El Garrafon is the lighthouse of **Punta Sur**, the most southern point of the island. A path leads past the lighthouse to a small Mayan ruin perched on the very edge of the cliff. This is a spectacular spot; the Caribbean surf pounds the headland, charter boats troll for big fish in the deep, dark-blue waters off the point where the current swirls around, and the hotels of Cancún shimmer in a long, low line on the horizon.

Even Isla Mujeres is not peaceful enough for some. If you're looking for real seclusion, consider a boat trip to **Isla Contoy**. This uninhabited island lies 15 miles (24 km) north of Isla Mujeres and has been preserved by the Mexican government as a national park and bird sanctuary. Only 4 miles (6 km) long by half a mile (0.8 km) wide, Contoy is a reminder of what Isla Mujeres and Cancún once looked like – a patchwork of mangrove, lagoons, sand dunes, sea, palm groves, coral and bush. The ranger station has a small museum explaining the various habitats and wildlife. Pelicans, frigate birds, terns and cormorants all nest on the island, and flamingos and spoonbills can also be found. In summer, turtles crawl ashore to lay their eggs in the sand. Boat trips from both Isla Mujeres and Playa Linda in Cancún include snorkelling and fishing in the clear waters around Contoy. Check with a travel agent for more details.

Cozumel

Pop. 60,000

Cozumel's superb coral reefs, immortalized on film by Jacques Cousteau in the 1950s, have made the island a place of pilgrimage for scuba divers from all over the world. However, many centuries before the crew of the *Calypso* began to explore the undersea world of Palancar Reef, Cozumel was a place of pilgrimage for the ancient Maya. Known to them as *Ah Cuzamil Peten* (the place of swallows), the island's temples **31** were dedicated to Ix Chel, the goddess of fertility, and people came from hundreds of miles around to worship at her shrine.

Cozumel was discovered by the Spaniard Juan de Grijalva in 1518, while he was sailing from Cuba to the Yucatán. On the site of present-day San Miguel, he and his crew held the first Christian mass in central America. A year later, Cortés followed, laying waste to the native shrines and spreading disease among the population. By the 17th century the island was practically uninhabited, and it became a useful hideaway for pirates such as Jean Lafitte and the Welsh-born buccaneer Henry Morgan, who later became Governor of Jamaica. It was only in the aftermath of the Caste Wars in the 1840s that the island was resettled by people fleeing from the mainland; these became the ancestors of today's *Cozumeleños*.

Modern-day Cozumel is a bit like Cancún and the Yucatán in miniature. It has modern hotels (but not too many), beautiful beaches (but not too crowded), just enough nightlife and plenty of shopping. There are also acres of jungle, miles of deserted coastline and a few small Mayan archaeological sites for good measure, all squeezed into an island just 33 miles (53 km) long by 9 miles (14 km) wide. And as if that wasn't enough, some of the best snorkelling and scuba diving anywhere in the world is to be had here.

The ferry from Playa del Carmen deposits you right in the heart of the only town on

*S*unbathers take the opportunity to cool off with a drink in the shade of a palapa bar.

the island, **San Miguel de Cozumel**. Directly opposite the pier is the main square, the Plaza del Sol, also known as the *zócalo*. The streets are laid out on a grid pattern – *avenidas* (avenues) run north to south, parallel to the coast and are intersected by east to west *calles* (streets), with even numbers to the north of the plaza, odd numbers to the south. The principal streets are Avenida Benito Juárez, also called the *Transversal*, which runs from the ferry pier across the north end of the plaza and continues all the way to the east coast of the island; and Avenida Rafael Melgar, the *Malecón*, which runs along the waterfront.

The plaza bustles with constant activity, surrounded by restaurants, small hotels, pavement cafés and shops. In the evenings the crowds migrate from the shops to the restaurants, bars and nightclubs. Once a week the plaza is reclaimed by the locals: on Sunday evenings the square

Gentle Giants of the Sea

The warm waters off the coast of the Yucatán were once home to countless thousands of sea turtles, the females returning year after year to the same sandy beaches where they were born to laboriously dig their nests and lay their clutches of up to 200 eggs. But years of relentless hunting and nest raiding have led to the green turtle (source of turtle soup), the loggerhead turtle and the beautiful hawksbill turtle (whose carapace is highly sought after as ornamental tortoise-shell) being declared endangered species. Turtle eggs are deemed a great delicacy and, despite laws which impose large fines for egg stealing, each year the beaches of Cozumel and the Yucatán are raided by poachers. Conservation schemes have been set up, involving beach patrols to monitor nest sites, and hatcheries where the eggs can be hatched in safety before returning the young turtles to the sea. Only time will tell if these efforts will be rewarded.

fills up with *Cozumeleños*, dressed in their Sunday best, who come to stroll, meet friends, exchange news, and dance to the music of one of the island bands.

Before exploring the rest of the island, you should pay a visit to the **Museo de la Isla de Cozumel**. The ground floor exhibits provide an interesting introduction to the geography and wildlife of Cozumel, from the luxuriant jungles of the interior to the splendid fringing coral reefs. The accompanying descriptions, in Spanish and English, are concise and well written, and highlight the islanders' concern for the environment. Upstairs the exhibits concentrate on Cozumel's long and varied history, with displays of Mayan pottery and sculpture, objects retrieved from the wrecks of Spanish galleons, and

even an early aqualung used during Cousteau's first explorations of the island's underwater marvels.

Between May and September the museum operates a turtle conservation project. Teams of volunteers monitor the beaches where the female turtles lumber ashore to dig their nests in the sand. The eggs are collected as soon as they are laid and taken to a hatchery where they will be safe from predators and human raiders.

The young turtles are returned to the sea once they have hatched. As a visitor you are invited to take part. A slide presentation at 9 p.m. is followed by a bus trip out to one of the beaches on the east coast where you can watch the turtles digging their nests and laying their eggs. You then help the conservation team to collect eggs or release newly hatched babies. Ask at the museum for details.

A coastal strip of hotel development stretches for a few miles to the north and south of San Miguel, culminating to the north in a dirt road that continues for a few miles to the scrubby shores of Bahía de Abrigo. There is not much to see here apart from sea birds, and the beckoning beaches of **Isla de Pasión** in the middle of the bay. This pretty island is a state-run nature reserve, with good snorkelling and birdwatching facilities, and can be

*S*norkellers at Chankanaab can spot colourful tropical fish, like this blue-striped grunt (inset). **35**

visited by a boat trip from San Miguel.

If you head south from town, you will soon see the International Pier, where the big cruise ships tie up. Just in front of the pier is **La Ceiba beach**, which is near to the hotel of the same name. The hotels here cater mainly for divers, and a number of diving shops and schools are to be found along the waterfront. Good diving and snorkelling can be enjoyed straight off the beach. A rocky shelf about 10 ft (3 m) deep slopes down to a sandy bottom in 25 ft (8 m) of water, with several small coral heads teeming with fish – among them butterfly fish, cardinals, beaugregories, Spanish hogfish, rock beauties, angelfish, and parrotfish.

If you swim straight out 50 yds (50 m) from the little pier in front of La Ceiba Hotel, you will find the wreckage of a small airliner lying on its back – there is usually a small buoy marking the wreck. This isn't the grisly scene of some disaster – it was dumped here as an underwater film set in 1977.

About 5 miles (8 km) from San Miguel is **Chankanaab Park**, where a rock-rimmed salt water lagoon has been made the centrepiece of a wildlife park. The lagoon is connected to the sea by a series of caves, and its crystal clear waters form a natural aquarium. Shady botanical gardens have been planted around the lagoon, containing over 300 species of plant from countries around the Caribbean, the haunt of birds, lizards and iguanas. Nearby is a small museum with displays of underwater photographs taken in the park. The sandy beach has sun-loungers, parasols, toilets, changing rooms, showers, lockers, a bar-restaurant, and four diving shops offering equipment hire and lessons. The snorkelling is excellent, and if you have never dived before, this is a good spot in which to learn.

Getting into the water couldn't be easier – steps have been carved out of the rock, and there are wooden handrails. The shallow rocky shelf near the shore is home to a marine garden of plant-like gorgonians and lacy, purple sea-fans, sloping down to a sandy bottom in about 15 ft (5 m) of water. There are small coral heads alive with fish, and for added interest the park authorities have dotted the sand with encrusted old cannons, a Chac Mool sculpture, a sunken fishing boat, and a 10-ft (3-m) statue of the Crucifixion!

The coast south of Chankanaab boasts some of the best bathing beaches on the island. **Playa San Francisco** and **Playa del Sol** have narrow strands of sparkling white sand squeezed between the sheltered water and a row of *palalpas*. Both have bars and restaurants, volleyball nets, jet skis, sailboats and snorkelling gear for hire. The beaches here, and the quieter stretches further south, are often visited by diving boats during the lunch break between dives on the reefs, which lie a short distance offshore. The chain of reefs – Paraíso, Yucab, Santa Rosa, Palancar, Punta Sur, Colombia, Maracaibo – was designated an underwater wildlife reserve (the **Parque Nacional Submarino de Palancar**) in 1980. Spear fishing and the removal of coral or any other living organisms from within the reserve is strictly forbidden.

Beyond the beaches, a side road on the left ends in a few miles at the farming village of **Cedral**, the only village on the island. Next door to the church is all that remains of Cozumel's oldest Mayan settlement, a crumbling vault atop a heap of stones, with a huge tree growing out of the roof. An agricultural fair, with livestock shows, a bullfight, music and dancing is held here each year at the beginning of May.

After the Cedral turn-off, the main road pulls away from the coast and cuts through thick jungle to reach the east coast at Playa Bush. The dirt road on the right leads in 3 miles (5 km) to lonely **Punta Celerain**, the southernmost tip of Cozumel. A lighthouse and a tiny Mexican Navy post are to be found here, and bored servicemen snooze in the shade while the lighthouse-keeper's hens and turkeys scratch about in the dust. Ask the keeper or one of **37**

his children to let you into the lighthouse. A sweaty climb up the steep spiral stairs will be rewarded with a wonderful view of the surf-pounded east coast stretching into the haze. To the left are the marshes surrounding the **Laguna de Colombia** – a paradise for bird-watchers but accessible only by boat – and you might try counting the number of diving boats bobbing about above the reefs.

Halfway between the lighthouse and the main road is the **Tumba del Caracol**, a small Mayan ruin dating from the late post-classic period, which may have served as a lighthouse. On the other side of the dunes lie 3 miles (5 km) of empty sandy beach, the perfect place to get away from it all. In fact, the entire length of Cozumel's east coast is a string of secluded beaches and craggy coves. The only signs of 'civilization' are the bar-restaurants

T he lighthouse at Punta Celerain, and (right) the majestic view from the top.

at the bathing beaches of Punta Chiqueros, Chen Rio and Punta Morena. Away from these spots you are advised to stick to sun-bathing and picnics – the surf on this coast creates a danger-ous undertow and there are no lifeguards to help you out: in most places there aren't even any other tourists.

At the lively beach bar called Mescalito you reach the east end of the Transversal, the cross-island road that leads back to San Miguel. A dirt road

continues along the coast for 15 miles (24 km) to the lighthouse at **Punta Molas**, offering the intrepid traveller equipped with a four-wheel drive vehicle the chance to explore rarely visited Mayan ruins, camp on deserted beaches, and dream of bucca-neers and buried treasure. The wrecks of several Spanish galleons have been discovered along this coast, and it is not unheard of to find pieces of boat, if not pieces of eight, washed up on the shore after

*A*ncient Mayan ruins rise from the jungle at San Gervasio.

at – mainly platforms and low walls or columns – the site is very atmospheric. Guided tours are available, or you can guide yourself using the guidebook on sale in San Miguel bookshops.

South to Tulum – Mexico's Caribbean Coast

100 miles of coastline and nearly 1000 years separate the cities of Cancún and Tulum, and it is only in the last two decades that a new road along the edge of the Caribbean has opened up the wild Quintana Roo coast to travellers. Popularly known as the Cancún–Tulum Corridor, this stretch of coast has many attractions for the tourist – superb beaches, offshore coral reefs, sleepy fishing villages, Mayan ruins, ultramodern resorts, beautiful *caletas* (inlets) and *cenotes* (caverns) and great diving and snorkelling. A regular bus service runs between Cancún and Tulum, but the best way to explore is to hire a car or jeep.

storms. (A word of warning – the insurance on rental vehicles may not cover you for driving on this road. Check your contract before heading into the sticks.)

Cozumel's best-preserved Mayan ruins are at **San Gervasio**, reached by a 6-mile (10-km) road leading north off the Transversal. Although the ruins **40** are not very impressive to look

The car ferry from Cozumel docks at the sleepy little village of **Puerto Morelos**. It's a bit of a backwater – the waterfront still shows signs of damage from Hurricane Gilbert, and grass grows through the cracks in the concrete of the village square, while pelicans preen themselves on the fishing boats tied up at the jetty. A new lighthouse rises above the crumbling remains of two earlier ones. But Puerto Morelos has a few pleasant restaurants, offshore is an excellent coral reef which attracts a regular flow of divers, and a visit to the town can make for an enjoyable change of pace. Back on the main road, about a mile before the Puerto Morelos road, is the **Crococun Crocodile Farm**, where you can watch the big crocodiles being fed. Local wildlife, such as *javelinas* (peccary, or wild pig) and deer, are also on view. Next door is

A big croc snoozes among the coconut palms at Crococun Crocodile Farm.

the rather scruffy and poorly presented Palancar Aquarium – not recommended.

Budding botanists should head for the **Alfredo Barrera Marin Botanical Garden** (*Jardin Botanico*), a 150-acre (61-ha) expanse of native tropical forest fringing a coastal mangrove swamp. You can potter about the back yard of a typical Mayan village hut, or seek out the *chiclero* camp, a reminder of the days when the sap of the zapote tree (*chicle*) was harvested to make chewing gum. Seven miles of peaceful forest trails provide fertile territory for bird-watchers and entomologists, winding among native Yucatecan species such as the chit palm (used by the Mayans to make their thatched huts), the *guaya* and the noble *ramon*.

A twisty road consisting of 3 miles (5 km) of rocks and potholes leads from the main road to the beautiful beach at **Punta Bete**. There is good snorkelling off the beach, and the bungalow-style accommodation is usually fully booked by visiting divers. There are campgrounds for tents and trailers, but backpackers travelling light make do with a hammock slung between a couple of coconut palms.

Playa del Carmen is the departure point for the passenger ferry to Cozumel. You can still detect some of the fishing village ambience that made this small town a haven for hippy travellers in the 1970s, but it's fading fast. The developers have discovered that the beaches here are just as good as Cancún's, and new hotels and condominiums are sprouting along the shoreline, pushing the nudist beach further and further north. Nevertheless, Playa is a pleasantly relaxed kind of place, the sort that encourages you to while away the whole afternoon lounging on the sand or sipping beer beneath the palms.

More than 1000 years before the ferries began to ply from Playa del Carmen, huge dugout canoes regularly set sail from the Mayan port of Pole a few miles to the south, carrying pilgrims bound for Cozumel and the shrines of Ix Chel, the Mayan goddess of fertility and medicine. The natural limestone harbour and ruined Mayan buildings of Pole are now part of **Xcaret**, a private ranch that has been developed as an 'eco-archaeological park'. There is a unique underground river excursion, along which you can swim for nearly 600 yds (600 m) through limestone caves and tunnels connecting the *cenote* to the salt water lagoon. Snorkellers can explore the emerald waters of the lagoon or cruise among the fish in the *caleta*.

The big attraction for visitors to **Pamul** is to watch the turtles that lumber onto the nearby beaches on summer

*P*assengers from Cozumel disembark amid the inviting, turquoise waters off Playa del Carmen.

*T*he limestone channels and caves at Xcaret offer a unique underground expedition for visiting snorkellers. Tame dolphins (above right) provide a less strenuous diversion.

nights to lay their eggs, and, a few weeks afterwards, the spectacle of thousands of newly hatched 'turtlets' making their life-or-death dash back into the sea. The tiny turtles must run the gauntlet of sea birds and other predators on their hazardous journey from nest to ocean – you can get some idea of the mortality rate from the fact that a female must lay up to 200 eggs to have a chance of one or two offspring surviving to maturity. Outside the turtle nesting season (July and August), the cove at Pamul offers the classic Caribbean combination of sunbathing, swimming and snorkelling. The water here is safe for children, sheltered by an offshore reef.

Perhaps the new, purpose-built resort of **Puerto Aventuras** offers a glimpse of the future for this rapidly developing coastline. It provides luxury accommodation in hotels and time-share condominiums clustered around a marina, golf course, diving school and beach-club complex, and is already offering serious competition to Cancún.

Anyone interested in the undersea world should pay a visit to the **Museo CEDAM** (*Club de Exploracion y Deporte Acuatico de Mexico*), a museum of underwater archaeology and exploration. The exhibits include cannons, coins and crockery retrieved by divers from the many wrecks that litter the treacherous offshore reefs, a gallery of stunning photographs of cave diving, and displays of objects found at the Mayan archaeological site of Xel-Há. Some of the exhibits in the museum have been raised from the wreckage of the Spanish galleon, the *Matanceros*, which sank in 1741 on a reef near **Akumal**. The reef and its wrecks have drawn divers to the site for many years, and the long beach at Akumal has grown into **45**

a low-key resort frequented by underwater adventurers and laid-back sun worshippers. The hotels and their guests have gradually displaced the turtles that once nested here in their thousands – Akumal is a Mayan name meaning 'the place of the turtle' – but the coconut groves planted by the natives survive in a fringe of palms along the beach. You can swim safely in the sheltered waters behind the reef, but for a little more seclu-sion take your snorkel gear and walk along the shore to the north of Akumal for about 20 minutes to reach **Yal-Ku**, a lovely, jungle-fringed inlet.

There is little to choose between the charms of **Kante-nah**, **Chemuyil** and **Xcacel** – all are picture-postcard combi-nations of alabaster sands lapped by azure waves. Xcacel has the added attraction of a sunken wreck off the southern point of the bay.

The jungle-fringed inlet at Xel-Há (below and right) is a huge, natural aquarium.

The scenic inlet at **Xel-Há**, now a national park, pulls in hundreds of day trippers from Cancún. A system of shallow, interconnected, crystal-clear lagoons (Xel-Há means 'clear water') has created a vast

natural nursery for many species of fish, but the ever-increasing number of snorkellers threatens to destroy the delicate environment. The park regulations now ask that visitors do not feed the fish, and snorkellers must keep within a designated area. Bathers should not go into the water while wearing suntan lotion, as the chemicals contained in it can harm the marine life.

Freshwater springs from underground streams mingle with the warm salt water to make a shimmering halocline, or mixing layer, that takes the appearance of an underwater heat haze. Numerous caves dot the limestone shore – one of them conceals a Mayan shrine – and drowned tunnels connect the sea with *cenotes* and sinkholes further inland. One rocky basin near the park entrance has been set aside as a natural aquarium, where non-swimmers can watch the fish. Above water, you can hike along the jungle paths which wind around the many-fingered fringes of the inlet and out to the rocky **48** seashore – but get there early if

you want to avoid the crowds. There are changing rooms, showers, lockers and cafés in the park.

The *caleta* of Xel-Há is the largest on Mexico's Caribbean coast, and like the one at Xcaret it was used as a harbour by the Mayas. Across the road from the national park is the recently excavated **archaeological site** of Xel-Há, the remains of a Mayan port and trade centre. The most interesting ruins are about 10 minutes' walk from the main road, clustered around the far end of a beautiful, wooded *cenote*.

The ancient walled city of **Tulum** attracts more visitors than any other Mayan site in the Yucatán, but the crowds cannot detract from the breathtaking beauty of the place. The name Tulum means 'fenced' or 'walled', a reference to the city's defences, but in pre-Hispanic times the city was

*T*he city of Tulum was dedicated to the worship of the 'Descending God' (insert)

called Zama, probably a corruption of 'zamal', to dawn. What better name for such a magnificent site than 'City of the Dawn'?

Tulum flourished in the late post-classic period (AD 1200-1513) as an important centre of trade, as shown by the objects found on the site by archaeologists: ceramics and flint from the interior of the peninsula, copper bells and rings from central Mexico, jade and obsidian from Guatemala.

Tulum was also a ceremonial centre dedicated to the worship of a deity known to us as the Descending God, whose image appears on many of Tulum's temples. The city seems to have been abandoned shortly after

*N*iches containing carvings of the mysterious 'Descending God' adorn the façade of the Temple of the Frescoes.

the Spaniards arrived in the 16th century. The Maya made the ruined city their home once more during the Caste War of the late 19th century, when Tulum became a sanctuary for the rebellious Chan Santa Cruz Indians, who were fighting for independence from Mexico. These fierce rebels and their **50** descendants maintained a veil of fear and mystery over the walled city until well into the 20th century. The airstrip and the new coast road from Cancún to Chetumal has made the site accessible: today's invaders arrive in air-conditioned coaches to trade dollars for souvenirs.

The city walls still stand, with watchtowers at each corner and narrow gates to north and south. You enter the site through the gate in the landward wall, and immediately **El Castillo** grabs your attention. Climb to the top for an excellent view of the ruins. The summit temple with its columns decorated with feathered serpents, a sign of Toltec influence, faces west. Above the door is a carving of the Descending God, a winged figure apparently diving towards the earth. The significance of this figure is unknown – he may represent the setting sun, the planet Venus, or the honey bee (honey was a much-valued commodity in the Yucatán).

On one side of El Castillo stands a plain little building which appears all aslant. This is the **Temple of the Descending God**, named after the image carved above the door.

Between El Castillo and the entrance gate lies the **Temple of the Frescoes**, which is probably the most interesting of Tulum's buildings. However, you will have to admire it from a distance, as pressure of numbers has led the authorities to fence it off for fear of damage.

Like the temple on the Castillo, this temple faces west, and is decorated with stucco masks of some deity, possibly Kukulcán, on the corners, and a representation of the Descending God in the central niche above the door. On the upper storey to the left of the door you can see red handprints on the wall. This motif appears in many Mayan sites, but its significance remains a mystery.

Many other smaller buildings and ruins are also there to explore, but if clambering about the ruins becomes too hot and tiring, you can always cool off with a swim from the sandy beach in the cove below the Castillo, where the Maya used to haul out their canoes.

Inland from Tulum about 26 miles (42 km), hidden deep in the forest, lies the most remote of the Yucatán's ruined cities: **Cobá**.

Beautifully situated on the shores of Lakes Cobá and Macanxoc, Cobá may be one of the largest archaeological sites in all Mexico. Initial surveys have revealed around 20,000 structures spread over an area of **51**

39 square miles (100 square km). An extensive network of local and regional *sacbes* ('white roads') has been discovered, with one reaching 63 miles (100 km) to Yaxuna, near Chichén Itzá. Cobá reached its peak during the period AD 800-1000, and declined through the succeeding centuries. Its size and sophisticated road network attest to the important position the city must have held in the ancient world.

Excavations did not begin until 1972, and very little has

so far been uncovered. At Cobá you can experience something of what the original archaeologists must have felt, as you wander through dense forest, the silence broken only by the hum of insects and the sharp calls of birds, with mysterious mounds of overgrown masonry looming out of the leaves. Potential explorers should come equipped with comfortable walking shoes, as more than a mile (1.5 km) separates the principal sights.

The entrance to the archaeological zone lies on the shore of Lake Cobá. The first place to head for is the **Iglesia**. Take the path to the right, signposted 'Grupo Cobá', just inside the entrance. Although Iglesia means 'church', this is actually a 90 ft (27 m) high pyramid, overgrown on all sides except one. Its name comes from the local people who light candles and offer flowers and incense

*A*n overgrown and secluded stela, and the great pyramid of Nohoch Mul at Cobá.

here, praying for good harvests. A steep and awkward scramble leads to the summit – no manicured Chichén Itzá-style masonry here – and an expansive view over the lakes and jungle. To the north east rises the silvery cone of Nohoch Mul, while other uncovered structures show as lumps beneath the carpet of jungle.

Return to the main path and follow it for about 20 minutes, keeping an eye out for parrots and toucans in the dense surrounding forest, and you'll arrive at the great pyramid called **Nohoch Mul**, meaning 'big hill'. Nohoch Mul is the biggest pyramid in northern Yucatán – at 138 ft (42 m) it tops the Temple of the Magician at Uxmal (114 ft, 35 m) and Chichén Itzá's Castillo (100 ft, 30 m). A sweaty climb up the 120 steps leads to a small temple on the top. Above the doorway you will recognize an image of the Descending God, also seen at Tulum and Sayil.

On the way back, turn left to visit the **Paintings Group** (*Conjunto de las Pinturas*). Here a small pyramid rises **53** above a colonnaded plaza, with a building at the top which retains traces of painted stucco above its lintel. Beyond, the path joins a *sacbe* leading to the Macanxoc group, where a number of *stelae* (carved pillars) and overgrown remains lie hidden in dense jungle.

You should allow at least half a day to explore Cobá, allowing time for a swim in one of the lakes. There are small restaurants near the car-park, and a good hotel nearby.

West to Mérida: Chichén Itzá, Uxmal, and the Cities of the Puuc

Highway 180 leads west from Cancún towards the city of Mérida, the Spanish colonial capital of the Yucatán. As soon as you leave the outskirts of Cancún, you are in another world. The road runs straight and narrow, with the jungle rising straight up from the edge of the tarmac. Occasionally you will pass the clearing of a *rancho*, or a small village of traditional thatched houses, where little Mayan children will run out to sell you fruit as you slow down to cross the *topes* (speed bumps) that mark the limits of each settlement.

Eventually the road blunders into the bustling, dusty town of Valladolid, founded in 1543 by Francisco de Montejo. Here you can visit the **Catedral de San Gervasio**, on the Zócalo, and the Yucatán's oldest church, San Bernardino de Siena, which dates from 1552. The town is also the home of the local honey-and-anise liqueur, *xtabentún*.

If the drive from Cancún has left you feeling hot and sticky, turn left a mile or so beyond Valladolid on the road to Dzitnup, to sample some indoor swimming, Yucatán style. The **Cenote Xkeken** (also known as the Cenote Dzitnup) is a natural underground swimming hole, its clear green water spectacularly lit by a shaft of sunlight shining through a single hole in the roof of the cavern. It's a popular bathing spot with local school children, and worth a visit even if you don't fancy a dip.

Yet another subterranean attraction lies a few miles before Chichén Itzá. The **Balankanché Caves** (*Grutas de Balankanché*) were rediscovered in 1959, having been abandoned by the Maya over 800 years ago. The guided tour of the caves leads down into a long humid cavern carved by an underground stream, past beautiful limestone formations to a large chamber where a huge stalagmite and stalactite have merged to form a tree-like pillar. Here the ancients left offerings of nearly 100 incense burners made of stone and pottery, dedicated to Tlaloc, the Toltec god of rain, water and the underworld. The cave ends at an underground lake a little farther on, where there is another group of offerings, this time of small *metates* (grinding stones). Tours in English run daily at 11 a.m., 1 p.m. and 3 p.m.

CHICHÉN ITZA

The city of Chichén Itzá was founded about AD 500, and flourished intermittently until AD 1200, when it was abandoned for reasons unknown. It reached its peak during the post-classic period, from AD 950-1200, when war-like Toltec invaders from central Mexico made the city their capital. The architectural and religious influences that the Toltecs brought with them – the use of columns, the reclining 'Chac Mool' sculptures, murals and low-reliefs of Toltec warriors and of jaguars and eagles devouring human hearts, and the cult of Kukulcán, the Feathered Serpent – are everywhere evident in the buildings of Chichén Itzá, side by side with traditional Mayan motifs such as the ubiquitous masks of the rain-god, Chaac. The Toltecs appear to have abandoned the city around AD 1200, but no one knows why.

At around this time, a Mayan tribe called the Itzá were driven from their home near present-day Champoton on the Campeche coast, and wandered through the Yucatán jungle, first south to Lake Peten Itzá in northern Guatemala, **55**

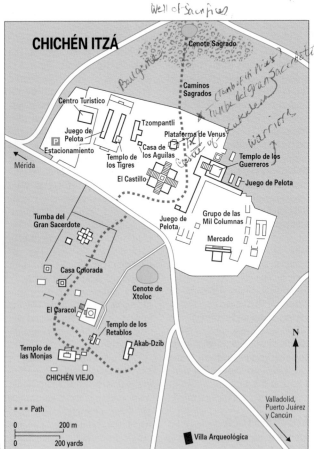

CHICHÉN ITZÁ

Well of Sacrifices

Cenote Sagrado

Ballgame

Caminos Sagrados

(Tomb of the Priest?)
Tumba del Gran Sacerdote

Centro Turistico

Tzompantli

Plataforma de Venus

Juego de Pelota

Casa de los Aguilas

Templo de los Guerreros

Castle of Kukulcán

Mérida

Estacionamiento

Templo de los Tigres

El Castillo

warriors

Juego de Pelota

Templo de los Guerreros

Juego de Pelota

Tumba del Gran Sacerdote

Grupo de las Mil Columnas

Casa Colorada

Cenote de Xtoloc

Mercado

El Caracol

Templo de los Retablos

Akab-Dzib

Templo de las Monjas

CHICHÉN VIEJO

N

Valladolid, Puerto Juárez y Cancún

- - - Path

0   200 m
0   200 yards

Villa Arqueológica

then north along the Caribbean coast to arrive at the deserted Toltec city some time in the mid 13th century. It was this tribe who gave the city its name (Chichén Itzá means 'Mouth of the Well of the Itzá'), and who founded the nearby city of Mayapan, near Mérida, which became the capital of Yucatán until revolt and civil war in the 15th century led to the decline of Mayan civilization. Chichén was deserted again, and the Itzá fled back to Lake Peten Itzá, where their new city of Tayasal flourished in the wilderness. Tayasal did not fall to the invading Spaniards until 1697.

A rash of advertising billboards by the roadside announces the approach to Chichén Itzá, the largest and most famous Mayan city in the Yucatán. Hordes of trippers descend upon the site every day, but the best way to enjoy Chichén is to stay overnight at one of the nearby hotels, so that you can watch the sun sink into the jungle from the top of El Castillo and explore the ruins at your leisure in the relative cool of the morning.

At the reception area next to the car park a scale model of the ancient city helps you to get your bearings, and to appreciate the size of Chichén Itzá in its heyday – the city extended way beyond the limits of the restored area that is visible today. Each evening there is a rather melodramatic **Sound and Light Show** (in Spanish at 7 p.m., in English at 9 p.m.). Coloured floodlights illuminate the ruins while a dramatized account of Mayan history and beliefs booms into the night.

The first thing you see as you enter the site is the imposing bulk of **El Castillo**, the **Temple of Kukulcán**. Nine superimposed platforms form a square pyramid 100 ft (30 m) high, topped with a rectangular temple. Steep staircases run up each of the four sides. The north and west faces have been completely restored, and if you have a head for heights you can climb to the top for a splendid view over the ruins and the green sea of jungle all around. On the temple door jambs are carvings of Toltec warriors, including one on the right hand **57**

The Mayan Calendar and Numbering System

The numbering system devised by the Maya had only three symbols: a dot for one, a horizontal bar for five, and a shell for zero. The system was vigesimal (based on the number 20), with groups of units, twenties, four hundreds (20 × 20), eight thousands (20 × 20 × 20) and so on. Thus the decimal number 8206 would be written as one dot over a shell over two bars over a dot and a bar, which means six units, plus ten twenties, plus no four-hundreds, plus one eight-thousand.

If you think the numbering system was complicated wait until you try to get to grips with the Mayan calendar! A cycle of 260 days (sometimes called the *tzolkin*) was made by combining 20 named days with the numbers 1 to 13. Each day in this cycle had its own fateful associations, and the tzolkin was used mostly in divination and fortune-telling. Then there was the 365-day Vague Year, made up of 18 named months of 20 days each, plus a five-day period of evil omen. This was meshed with the tzolkin to produce a cycle called the Calendar Round, which repeated itself every 52 years, or 18,980 days. This was not good enough to deal with the long time periods involved in history, astronomy and genealogy, in which the Maya were deeply interested, so for these purposes a system called the Long Count was used, which expressed a particular date in terms of the number of days elapsed since a starting point, or 'beginning of time', which is thought to correspond to 13 August 3114 BC. Long Count dates used the vigesimal system described above, but (just to be difficult) substituted 18 for 20 in the second column. The periods used in the Long Count were the *kin* (one day); *uinal* (20 days); *tun* (18 uinals or 360 days); *katun* (20 tuns, 7200 days); and *baktun* (20 katuns, 144,000 days). Dates were written in descending order, so the Long Count date 9.11.0.5.9, which appears on a monument found at Cobà, records a date (9 × 144,000) + (11 × 7200) + (0 × 360) + (5 × 20) + 9 = 1,375,309 days after the base date, which corresponds to a day in AD 653.

side of the main door of a bearded warrior, which may represent Kukulcán himself.

The construction of the pyramid betrays the Mayan obsession with time measurement. The four staircases, facing the four points of the compass, have 91 steps – four multiplied by 91 (plus the platform on top) equals 365, the number of days in the year. Looking at each face, there are nine tiers on each side of the staircase, making 18, the number of months in the Mayan year. Inset into the tiers are 52 panels, the number of years in the cycle of the Mayan Calendar Round.

El Castillo reveals its most striking secret only twice a year, during the spring and autumn equinoxes (21 March and 22 September). On and around these days the setting sun casts the shadow of the pyramid's north-western corner onto the balustrade of the northern staircase. The wavy shadow combines with the stone serpent's head at the foot of the staircase to give the appearance of a huge, sunlit snake slithering down from the temple towards the Sacred Cenote. Thousands of visitors come to witness the show, and the hotels are booked solid for these dates 12 months in advance.

In 1931 archaeologists tunnelled into the base of the pyramid to see if there were any earlier structures beneath. They discovered a stone box which contained bones, flint daggers, jade and turquoise, and beyond, a flight of steps which led to a small, buried temple. The chamber within yielded a beautifully preserved statue of Chac Mool and a red-painted effigy of a jaguar with eyes of jade and teeth of flint. The narrow, low-roofed tunnel remains, and you can follow it and the constricted, slippery stairs to the buried temple, but if you suffer from claustrophobia, give it a miss. The entrance is at the foot of the northern staircase, open between 11 a.m. and 3 p.m.

West from El Castillo is the **Ball Court** (*Juego de Pelota*), the biggest and best preserved in all Central America. The vertical walls that line the **59**

ceremonial playing field are 27 ft (8 m) high, 272 ft (83 m) long, and stand 99 ft (30 m) apart. The lower parts are decorated with carved feathered serpents and low-reliefs showing uniformed ball players. At the halfway line, the carvings depict the captain of one team holding his opponent's severed head while gouts of blood spurt from the neck of the loser. Or

60

winner, perhaps: some scholars have suggested that it was the winning captain who had the honour of sacrificing his life to the gods, though this could hardly have been much of an incentive to win! The noise during play must have been extraordinary as the walls act like an echo chamber. If you stand on the platform at one end of the court, you can hear someone speaking at the other end quite clearly, and if you stand beneath one of the scoring rings and shout or clap, the echo bounces back and forth several times before dying away.

*T*he grim faces of Mayan gods gaze out over magnificent El Castillo, at Chichén Iteá.

The tall building on the east side of the Ball Court, facing El Castillo, is the **Temple of the Jaguars** (*Templo de los Jaguares*), so named for the carvings of the big cats on the upper walls. The upper chamber, guarded by two huge feathered serpents, contains carvings of warriors and beautiful frescoes of battle scenes. The lower chamber, at ground level, houses a statue of a jaguar, similar in style to the one found in the buried temple beneath El Castillo. The column to its left bears a carving thought to represent a Mayan creation myth. At the base of the pillar is the face of a god, with tears streaming out to form the waters of the world, from which grow fish and a turtle. A serpent, symbol of fertility, sprouts from the top of the god's head and twines about the human figure above. The walls of the chamber are decorated with carvings of warriors in procession, some of which still retain traces of their original painted colours – red, blue, yellow and green. In the centre of the rear wall is a bearded figure which may represent Kukulcán.

Next to the Temple of the Jaguars lies the chilling **Tzompantli**, or **Platform of the Skulls**. The walls of this T-shaped platform are decorated with row upon row of human skulls, apparently skewered on poles. Similar platforms were used in Aztec cities to display the severed heads of enemies, and it is possible that the Toltecs of Chichén Itzá, predecessors of the Aztecs of central Mexico, used this one for the **61** same purpose. Perhaps the luckless losers from the neighbouring Ball Court also ended up here.

Two more stone platforms lie nearby. **The Platform of Eagles and Jaguars** is adorned with carvings of the said beasts clutching human hearts in their claws, while the **Platform of Venus** is named after the stars carved at its corners, thought to represent the planet Venus. These may have served as stages for religious rites.

At this point, a 330 yd (300 m) ceremonial road leads from El Castillo to the **Sacred Cenote** (*Cenote Sagrada*), also known as the Well of Sacrifice. This is 65 yds (60 m) in diameter, and the overgrown walls drop vertically for 70 ft (21 m) from rim to water level. For the Maya, this sinister sink-hole was not, as with other *cenotes*, a source of drinking water, but the home of Chaac, the rain god. In times of drought, Chaac was appeased with human sacrifices, thrown alive into the eerie depths along with offerings of precious objects. Underwater archaeologists exploring

---

The Ball Game

The ball game is a very ancient rite – reliefs of ball players have been found in Olmec sites dating from before the birth of Christ – and it was still being played by the Aztecs when the Spaniards arrived in the 16th century. Ball courts have been found in ancient cities all over Mexico. The game was played by two opposing teams, who tried to strike a hard rubber ball through stone rings mounted in the side walls of the court.

Carvings show players wearing protective padding on hips, arms, left ankle and right knee, with a bat tucked in their waistband. That the game had religious significance is certain – indeed, the carvings on many courts, including that at Chichén Itzá, show that the captain of one team was sacrificed at the end of the game.

Dense jungle surrounds the colonnaded ruins of the imposing Temple of the Warriors.

the bottom of the *cenote* recovered numerous human bones and skulls (male and female, adult and child) and a rich haul of pots, figurines and jewellery. Some of these treasures can be seen at the Regional Museum of Anthropology in Mérida.

The colonnaded building to the north east of El Castillo is the **Temple of the Warriors** (*Templo de los Guerreros*),

which is a near-perfect copy of a pyramid found in the Toltec capital of Tula, 50 miles (80 km) north west of Mexico City. You enter the temple through a forest of square columns, all decorated with carvings of fierce-looking Toltec warriors, and ascend a flight of stairs to a large statue of Chac Mool. These typically Toltec sculptures show a reclining figure **63** holding a bowl on its belly, perhaps to hold incense burners during religious rituals, or even to receive the hearts of human sacrifices.

Take a look at the low-relief carvings on the walls to the right of the staircase, which depict a jaguar and a bear-like animal holding human hearts in their claws. The door behind the statue is framed by two huge, feathered serpents, their tail-rattles arched over their heads, guarding the entrance to the inner temple. Here an altar at the back is supported by *atlantes*, small statues of Toltec soldiers. The outside of the building is decorated with the elephant-nosed masks of Chaac, the Mayan rain god.

From the south side of El Castillo, a dirt path leads past a snack bar to a group of older buildings, where the Toltec influence is less marked. On the way you'll pass the **Tomb of the High Priest**, or Osario, an unrestored pile of rubble that was once a small pyramid. Within it were found five tombs containing human remains, built one on top of the other.

The lowest connected with a natural cave in the limestone beneath. A little farther on is **Chichan Chob**, or the **Red House** (*Casa Colorada*), a good example of earlier Puuc-style architecture, with its narrow doors (no columns here), plain lower walls and upper façade decorated with Chaac masks and geometric designs.

Unique among the ancient cities of the Yucatán is the building known as **El Caracol** or **The Observatory**. It was named El Caracol ('the snail') by the explorer John Lloyd Stephens in 1841, because its spiral construction reminded him of a snail's shell. The construction of this unusual building took place in stages over an interval spanning the late classic and early post-classic periods. The original circular tower shows typical Puuc features, including Chaac masks above the cornice. The rectangular platforms which surround it were added later, and the archaeologists have left open trenches so that you can see the various stages.

A Selection of Hotels and Restaurants in Cancún and Cozumel

Recommended Hotels

Cancun and Cozumel are resorts aimed mainly at the package-holiday market. As a result there is little to choose between hotels in the same price band when it comes to the quality of service and amenities offered. All hotels in Cancun's Hotel Zone have air-conditioned rooms with en suite bathrooms and balconies, swimming pools, restaurants and beach access. Independent travellers might like to try one of the hotels listed below, recommended by Berlitz.

Prices do not normally include breakfast, so check before you book. As a basic guide we have used the symbols below to indicate prices for a double room with bath or shower, including tax, during the high season.

Cancún:	I	below US$70
	II	US$70–150
	III	over US$150
Cozumel:	I	below US$50
	II	US$50–100
	III	over US$100

Cancún

Albergue CREA (Youth Hostel)   I
Km 2.5, Paseo Kukulcán,
Zona Hotelera, Cancún,
Q. Roo 77500 México.
Tel. (988) 83-13-37.

Cheapest accommodation in Cancún. Separate male and female dormitories. Has its own swimming pool.

Calinda   II
Km 4, Paseo Kukulcán,
Zona Hotelera, Cancún,
Q. Roo 77500 México.

Tel. (988) 83-16-00.
Fax. (988) 83-18-57.
Next to Marine Terminal.
Good location for watersports
and boats to islands.

Calinda Viva

Km 8, Paseo Kukulcán,
Zona Hotelera, Cancún,
Q. Roo 77500 México.
Tel. (988) 83-08-00.
Fax. (988) 83-20-87.
Good location with the beach
on one side and the busy Plaza
Caracol area just up the road.

Camino Real

Km 8.5, Paseo Kukulcán,
Zona Hotelera, Cancún,
Q. Roo 77500 México.
Tel. (988) 83-01-00;
(800) 228 3000.
Fax. (988) 83-17-30.
Great situation on the tip of
Punta Cancún.

Cancún Plaza

Km 18, Paseo Kukulcán,
Zona Hotelera, Cancún,
Q. Roo 77500 México.
Tel. (988) 85-00-72.

Fax. (988) 85-02-36.
Quiet, uncrowded location at
the south end of the Hotel
Zone.

Fiesta Americana Condesa

Km 15, Paseo Kukulcán,
Zona Hotelera, Cancún,
Q. Roo 77500 México.
Tel. (988) 85-10-00;
(800) FIESTA-1.
Fax. (988) 85-16-50.
Huge, thatched palapa over
lobby bar.

Hyatt Regency Cancún

Km 8.5, Paseo Kukulcán,
Zona Hotelera, Cancún,
Q. Roo 77500 México.
Tel. (988) 83-09-66;
(800) 228 9000.
Fax. (988) 83-13-49.
14-storey tower, near Plaza
Caracol.

Krystal Cancún

Km 8.5, Paseo Kukulcán,
Zona Hotelera, Cancún,
Q. Roo 77500 México.

Tel. (988) 83-11-33;
(800) 231 9860.
Fax. (988) 83-17-90.
Includes one of Cancún's top
nightclubs – Christine's.

Meliá Cancún   ▐▐▐
Km 15, Paseo Kukulcán,
Zona Hotelera, Cancún,
Q. Roo 77500 México.
Tel. (988) 85-11-14;
(800) 336 3542.
Fax. (988) 85-19-63.
Impressive architecture, huge
glass pyramid over lobby.

Oasis   ▐▐
Km 15.5, Paseo Kukulcán,
Zona Hotelera, Cancún,
Q. Roo 77500 México.
Tel. (988) 85-08-67;
(800) 44-OASIS.
Fax. (988) 85-01-31.
Hotel complex in beautifully
landscaped surroundings.

Plaza Kokai   ▐
Av. Uxmal 26,
Ciudad Cancún,
Q. Roo 77500 México.
Tel. (988) 84-32-18.
Fax. (988) 84-43-35.
Situated on a quiet side street,
close to the town centre. Pool.

Sheraton Cancún Resort   ▐▐▐
Km 12.5, Paseo Kukulcán,
Zona Hotelera, Cancún,
Q. Roo 77500 México.
Tel. (988) 83-19-88;
(800) 325 3535.
Fax. (988) 85-02-02.
Mayan ruins in hotel grounds.
Floodlit tennis courts.

Stouffer Presidente   ▐▐
Km 7, Paseo Kukulcán,
Zona Hotelera, Cancún,
Q. Roo 77500 México.
Tel. (988) 83-02-00;
(800) HOTELS-1.
Fax. (988) 83-25-15.
One of Cancún's first hotels,
ideally situated between the
golf course and the beach.

Cozumel

La Ceiba   ▐▐▐
Apdo. 284, Cozumel,
Q. Roo 77600 México.
Tel. (987) 2-08-16;
(800) 777 5873.
Right on the beach, near good
snorkelling. Has own pier.

El Cozumeleño ▮▮▮

Apdo. 53, Cozumel,
Q. Roo 77600 México.
Tel. (987) 2-01-49;
(800) 437 3923.
Fax. (987) 5-32-69.
Situated on the best beach north of town.

Galapago Inn ▮▮

Apdo. 289, Cozumel,
Q. Roo 77600 México.
Tel. (987) 2-06-63;
(800) 847 5708.
Attractive spot south of town. Offers diving package tours.

Meson San Miguel ▮

Av. Benito Juárez 2,
San Miguel, Cozumel,
Q. Roo 77600 México.
Tel. (987) 2-02-33.
Convenient location right on the Plaza, near the ferry pier.

El Pirata ▮

Av. 5 Sur,
San Miguel, Cozumel,
Q. Roo 77600 México.
Tel. (987) 2-00-52.
Small, clean, quiet, family-run hotel near the Plaza.

Playa Azul ▮▮

Apdo. 31, Cozumel,
Q. Roo 77600 México.
Tel. (987) 2-00-43;
(800) 528 1234.
Fax. (987) 2019-15.
Good value for beachfront accommodation.

Safari Inn ▮

Apdo. 51 Cozumel,
Q. Roo 77600 México.
Tel. (987) 2-06-61;
(800) 854 9334
Diver's waterfront hangout a few blocks south of the Plaza.

Sol Caribe ▮▮▮

Apdo. 259, Cozumel,
Q, Roo 77600 México.
Tel. (987) 2-07-00;
(800) FIESTA-1.
South of town, near the cruise liner pier and the beach.

Stouffer Presidente ▮▮▮

Cozumel, Q. Roo 77600 México. Tel. (987) 2-03-22; (800) HOTELS-1.
Fax. (987) 2-13-60.
Great location beside caleta (diving-boat harbour), and close to Chankanaab Park. **69**

The Fish Market ▉▉▉
Av. Cobá 12, downtown.
Tel. 84-41-80.
Choose your own seafood from the market-stall display and have it cooked to order.

La Fondue ▉▉
Av. Cobá at Calle Nube, downtown.
Tel. 84-16-97.
Elegant. French-style cuisine: fondue, steaks, seafood.

Garibaldi's ▉▉
Calle Azucenas 3, downtown.
No telephone.
Mexican food and music, lively party atmosphere.

Guadalajara Grill ▉▉
Km 9.5, Hotel Zone.
No telephone.
Lagoonside dining. Party atmosphere, live rock music later in the evenings.

La Habichuel ▉▉▉
C/Margaritas 25, downtown.
Tel. 84-31-58.
Classic Yucatecan cuisine, outdoor tables.

Hong Kong ▉▉
Av. Cobá 49, downtown.
No telephone.
Good Chinese cooking, choice of indoor or outdoor tables.

Jalapeños ▉
Km 6.5, Hotel Zone.
Tel. 83-28-96.
Stuffed chillies, tacos, seafood. Live reggae music.

Lorenzillo's ▉▉▉
Km 10.5, Hotel Zone.
Tel. 83-12-54.
Palapa-style restaurant built over the lagoon. Seafood restaurant.

El Méxicano ▉▉▉
La Mansion-Costa Blanca Mall, Km 8, Hotel Zone.
Tel. 83-22-20/84-12-72.
Top-notch Mexican restaurant, with a nightly show of traditional music and dance.

Recommended Restaurants

Cast aside your preconceptions about Mexican food and make the most of the opportunity to savour the local Yucatecan cuisine. The dishes are often subtle and exotic, influenced by the recipes of the ancient Maya. Fiery heat is an optional extra – chilli sauces are served on the side, so you can make your meat as hot or as mild as you like.

The best value and variety is to be found in downtown Cancún, where you can enjoy local food at a reasonable cost. For plush, stylish restaurants, international cuisine and high prices, stick to the Hotel Zone. In general, reservations are needed only in the more expensive hotel restaurants. Elsewhere it's first come, first served. Below is a list of restaurants recommended by Berlitz; if you find other places worth recommending we'd be pleased to hear from you.

As a basic guide we have used the following symbols to give some idea of the price of a three-course meal for two, excluding drinks:

I	below US$20
II	US$20-40
III	over US$40

Cancún

El Café ▌▌
Av. Nader 5, downtown.
Tel. 84-15-84.
Pleasant patio-café, popular with the locals.

Cenacolo ▌▌▌
Calle Claveles 26, downtown.
Tel. 84-15-91.
Sophisticated Italian cuisine; chic, romantic atmosphere.

100% Natural   ▌▌
Plaza Terramar, Km 8.5,
Hotel Zone.
Tel. 84-16-17.
Health food, lots of fresh fruit
and vegetables.

Pop   ▌
Av. Tulum, near Tourist
Office, downtown.
Tel. 84-19-91.
Good breakfast menu. Air-
conditioned restaurant or *al*
fresco patio.

Rolandi's   ▌▌
Av. Cobá 12, downtown.
Tel. 84-40-47.
Pizzas cooked on wood fire,
pasta, flaming desserts.

Cozumel

Café del Puerto   ▌▌
The Plaza, opposite the pier.
Tel. 2-03-16.
Seafood, grills, pasta dishes.
Dining room overlooks har-
bour.

Carlos'n'Charlie's   ▌▌
Av. Rafael Melgar.
Tel. 2-01-91.
American-style ribs and grills,
party atmosphere. You can
play table tennis and volleyball at the back.

Morgan's   ▌▌▌
On the Plaza.
Tel. 2-05-84.
Elegant, nautical decor, live
traditional music. Good sea-
food.

Pepe's Grill   ▌▌▌
Av. Rafael Melgar.
Tel: 2-02-13.
Dine by open windows look-
ing onto the sea. Steaks and
seafood.

Pizza Rolandi   ▌▌
Av. Rafael Melgar.
No telephone.
Pleasant, flower-fringed patio,
crisp pizzas from wood-fired
oven.

Plaza Leza   ▌
South side of the Plaza.
Tel. 2-10-41.
Friendly pavement cafe, good
for breakfast and lunch.

The tower has four doors which open into a circular chamber, and four inner doors which lead to a concentric inner chamber around a solid masonry core. From here a spiral staircase led to the (now ruined) upper chamber, where narrow windows allowed the Mayan astronomers to observe the movements of the sun, the moon and Venus.

Nearby lies the **Nunnery** (*La Casa de las Monjas*), named by the Spaniards because its many chambers reminded them of a convent. This large building has been remodelled and extended many times, and is riddled with exploratory tunnels dug by archaeologists looking for evidence of earlier stages of construction. The main point of

Early Adventurers

The names of Stephens and Catherwood are inextricably linked with the Yucatán. Their explorations brought to light the achievements of Mayan civilization, which had lain forgotten in the jungles of Central America for over 400 years.

The American John Lloyd Stephens (1805-1852) was a lawyer by training, but an 'Indiana Jones'-style adventurer-archaeologist by inclination. Spurred by reports of ruined cities in Central America and the Yucatán, he made two expeditions to the area in search of lost civilizations. He was accompanied by the British artist and architect Frederick Catherwood (1799-1854), whose drawings of the Mayan temples and palaces provoked a wave of popular interest throughout the world. Their experiences are vividly recounted in two works by Stephens, complete with Catherwood's illustrations: *Incidents of Travel in Central America, Chiapas and Yucatán*, (1841, two volumes), and *Incidents of Travel in Yucatán*, (1843, two volumes). These classic accounts of exploration are still in print, and make absorbing reading for travellers touring the archaeological sites around Cancún.

73

interest is the beautiful façade at the eastern end, an example of the Chenes style of architecture, in which decoration covers the entire wall.

The wall here is decorated all over with numerous Chaac masks and geometric designs, but look at it through half-closed eyes, and you will notice that it is also a huge face of Chaac. The panels at top right and left are the eyes, and the door is the mouth, lined with hooked teeth. The lintel is carved with hieroglyphics, and above is a panel depicting a seated figure sporting an elaborate head-dress, possibly a god.

Next door is the impressive ornamented **Iglesia** (church), another building in the Puuc tradition. Look closely at the western façade: on either side of the Chaac mask above the door are panels depicting human figures with animals on their backs – bee, snail, armadillo and turtle. These are thought to represent the four *bacabe*, the gods associated with the four directions of the compass, who hold up the sky according to Mayan mythology.

A short path leads to the rather plain building known as **Akab Dzib**, a Mayan name meaning 'writing in the dark'. Enter through the door in the south (short) side, and you will see why. You will find yourself in a dark chamber from which another door leads off. The lintel of this inner door is carved with hieroglyphics on the front (the 'writing in the dark'), while the underside of the lintel bears an image of a figure seated on a throne, apparently in the act of carrying out some ritual. These were the first hieroglyphics discovered in the Yucatán by Stephens and Catherwood in 1841. Today, 150 years later, their meaning is still a mystery.

MÉRIDA

Pop. 600,000
La Blanca Mérida – **Mérida**, the White City – is steeped in history. Founded by the Spanish conquistadors in 1542, on the site of the Mayan city of T'Ho, it grew rich from the 18th and 19th century maize and henequen plantations.

Hitch a ride on a horse-drawn calesa for a relaxing tour around the delights of Mérida.

Today it is capital of the state of Yucatán, and the peninsula's principal city.

The focal point is the **Plaza de la Independencia**, or Plaza Principal, the main square, where the locals congregate at weekends and in the evenings for a quiet stroll, a smoke, a shoe-shine, or a chat. Benches and *confidenciales* (S-shaped 'love-seats') sit in the shade of spreading laurel trees, inviting you to rest awhile and admire the colonial architecture which lines the plaza. The oldest building in Mérida is the **Palacio de Montejo**, on the south side of the square. The façade, which is the only remnant of the original building, dates from 1549, and carries a relief of two knights in armour standing on the heads of four cowed and naked Indians – the conquering Spaniards trampling the vanquished Maya underfoot. It is possible that the carving was executed by Mayan masons, as it adheres to the Toltec tradition of depicting victorious warriors standing on the heads of their defeated enemies. The rest of the palace, now occupied by a bank, dates from the 19th century. Go inside for a look around the beautiful courtyard (there is also a useful currency exchange kiosk here).

Opposite the Montejo palace is the late 19th century **Palacio del Gobierno** (Governor's Palace), where you can admire the mural paintings of local artist Fernando Castro Pacheco, depicting the history of the Yucatán people. On the east side of the square is the **Catedral**, one of the oldest in the Americas. It was begun in 1561, using stones from the ruins of T'Ho, the Mayan city that once stood on this site. Inside is the curious **Cristo de las Ampollos** ('Christ of the

Mayan history immortalized in stone at the Monumento de la Patria.

77

Blisters'), a crucifix supposedly carved in the 16th century from the wood of a miraculous tree that burned without being destroyed. The carving survived a later fire, but broke out in the blisters that give it its name. Facing the Catedral across the plaza is the clock tower of the **Palacio Municipal** (City Hall). The present colonial-style building, built in 1928, occupies the site of the original 16th century town hall. On Sundays you can enjoy open-air performances of Yucatecan folk dancing in front of the Palacio.

A short walk from the plaza leads to Mérida's **Mercado Municipal** (market), which lies a couple of blocks away at Calles 56 and 65. The market is a must for adventurous shoppers in search of local specialities such as hammocks, Panama hats, sandals, masks, *pinatas*, *huipiles* and *guayaberas*. Try to be there on weekend mornings for maximum atmosphere.

Make time for a stroll along Calle 60. This pleasant street leads north from the corner of **78** the plaza by the Catedral, pass-ing the lovely little **Parque Cepeda Peraza** on the right. The park is a shady nook of pavement cafés tucked between the 17th-century **Iglesia de Jesus** (Church of Jesus) and the colonial Grand Hotel. A little farther on is the **Teatro Péon Contreras**, a beautiful, restored turn-of-the-century theatre. To the right of the lobby is a useful tourist information office, open 8 a.m. to 9 p.m. Continue past the university on the left to the **Parque Santa Lucía**, where concerts of folk music are held on Thursday evenings at 9 p.m. The Iglesia de Santa Lucía, opposite, dates from 1575.

Continue right for two blocks at Calle 47 to reach the foot of the **Paseo Montejo**. This broad, tree-lined boulevard is a legacy of 19th-century Mérida's wealthy upper classes, who built their opulent mansions here in imitation of the elegant avenues of Paris. The most impressive is the Palacio Canton at the corner of Calle 43. Designed by the same architect as the Teatro Péon Contreras, and built from 1909-1911 for a famous general, it now houses the **Museo Regional de Antropología y Historia** (Regional Museum of Anthropology and History). This excellent museum contains displays of pottery, sculpture, jewellery and other artifacts found during excavations of Mayan ruins, including objects recovered from the Sacred Cenote of Chichén Itzá. The explanatory captions are mostly in Spanish, but English-speaking guides are available if needed.

The Paseo continues for a mile or so, past banks, airline offices, gardens, 19th-century mansions in varying states of repair and tempting pavement cafés, to the imposing **Monumento a la Patría** (Monument to the Fatherland), a 1950s 'Neo-Mayan' sculpture.

UXMAL

The region to the south of Mérida is known as the Puuc, a Mayan word meaning 'ridge of hills'. Travelling from Mérida towards the ancient city of Uxmal you meet the hills beyond the village of Muna, a long ridge which rises no more than a few hundred feet above the plain, but none the less notable in this vast, flat landscape. You will also notice that the land here in the north west of the peninsula supports more agriculture than in the east. The road from Mérida passes many farms, maize plantations and henequen ranches, and the area around nearby Oxkutzcab is the most important citrus fruit-growing area in Yucatán.

The henequen ranch at **Yaxcopoil**, 21 miles (34 km) south of Mérida on the road to Uxmal, is open to the public. A visit to this restored 17th-century *hacienda* and museum will reveal how the spiky henequen plant is converted into a useful natural fibre, and gives a glimpse into the day-to-day lives of plantation owners.

The fertility of the Puuc region is reflected in the name Uxmal, which may mean 'abundant harvest', although a more popular translation is 'thrice built'. Whatever its ancient name may have meant, to present-day visitors Uxmal means 'one of the most beauti- **79** ful of the ancient cities of the Yucatán'. The city flourished during the late classic period (AD 600-1000), producing the biggest and best of the Puuc style of architecture.

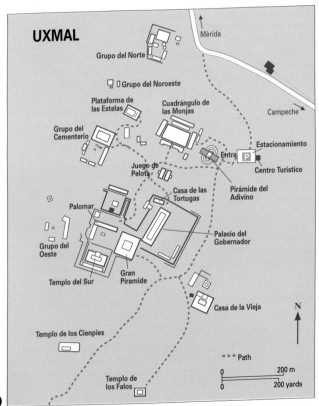

UXMAL

Grupo del Norte

Grupo del Noroeste

Plataforma de las Estelas

Cuadrángulo de las Monjas

Grupo del Cementerio

Entra

Estacionamiento

Centro Turistico

Juego de Pelota

Casa de las Tortugas

Pirámide del Adivino

Palomar

Palacio del Gobernador

Grupo del Oeste

Templo del Sur

Gran Pirámide

Templo de los Cienpies

Casa de la Vieja

Templo de los Falos

Mèrida

Campeche

N

■ ■ ■ Path

0   200 m
0   200 yards

There are a few hotels around the site, and the reception area has a restaurant, shops, and a small museum. There is a **Light and Sound Show** each evening (in Spanish at 7 p.m., English at 9 p.m.).

As you enter the site you pass a *chultún*, a circular rain-trap with a storage cistern beneath. The lack of *cenotes* and the depth to the water table at Uxmal meant that the city's population depended for their water supplies on the rain collected in these cisterns. The uncertainty of the water supply may have been the reason that Uxmal was repeatedly abandoned and re-occupied.

The Dwarf of Uxmal

In the 19th century a Spanish friar recorded a Mayan legend related to him by a native of Nohpat, near Uxmal. It was the story of an old witch who lived at Kabah, and her dwarf grandson.

One day the dwarf discovered a magical musical instrument that his grandmother had hidden beneath the ashes of the hearth. He played the instrument, and the sound struck terror into the heart of the evil king of Uxmal, for a prophecy had decreed that whoever played that instrument would himself become king.

So the king set the dwarf a challenge, to see who was stronger. Each would try to break a basketful of *cocoyoles* (a hard nut) on his head. The king thought this would kill the dwarf, and that his throne would be safe. But with his grandmother's help, the dwarf fashion\ed a helmet which he concealed beneath a wig, and survived the test. Furious, the king tried to crack the nuts on his own head, but fractured his skull and died. The dwarf was hailed by the people of Uxmal as a great magician, and he built a huge pyramid in celebration – the Pyramid of the Magician, or House of the Dwarf, and a home for his grandmother, the House of the Old Woman, which rises from the jungle to the east of the Palace of the Governor.

The **Pyramid of the Magician** (*Pirámide del Adivino*), also known as the House of the Dwarf, rises ahead of you. This pyramid is 114 ft (35 m) tall, higher than the Castillo at Chichén Itzá, and is unique in having an oval outline. Five stages of construction have been discovered, the most impressive of which is the western façade of 'Temple IV'.

This doorway sits on top of an extremely steep staircase bordered with Chaac masks, and is elaborately decorated in the Chenes style with faces of Chaac and plant motifs. 'Temple V', at the very top of the pyramid, is more simply ornamented with geometric designs.

From the summit you can enjoy the view of the archaeo-

logical site and the gently undulating plains stretching away to the horizon. Pick your way carefully down again and head for the **Nunnery Quadrangle** (*Cuadrangulo de las Monjas)*. The buildings here are the cream of Puuc-style architecture, their upper façades carved with intricate designs and representations of thatched huts, two-headed serpents, jaguars and the ubiquitous Chaac. To appreciate the care with which this square was laid out, sit on the top of the steps on the north (highest) side and look across at the south side.

The Pyramid of the Magician rises above the classical Mayan architecture of Uxmal.

Notice how the platform on which you are sitting coincides with the cornices on the buildings to your left and right, which in turn are in line with the roof of the building on the far side. The cornice on the far side is on the same level as the platforms to left and right, and the roofs to left and right are in line with the cornice behind you. These alignments give a feeling of harmony and balance, and testify to the aesthetic aspirations of the Mayan architects who designed it.

The main entrance to the quadrangle is an archway on the south side. Go down through the remains of a small ball court, and up to the magnificent **Palace of the Governor** (*Casa del Gobernador*), which sits atop two huge, superimposed, man-made platforms. The main façade – 330 ft (100 m) long – is divided into three parts by two tall, vaulted arches, and faces east towards the point on the horizon where the planet Venus rises. The upper part is decorated with Chaac masks in a sinuous wave pattern, and has a centrepiece showing a human figure seated on a throne wearing an elaborate feathered head-dress. The 11 doorways open into chambers whose roofs are home to colonies of bats; Stephens and Catherwood, on their visit to Uxmal in 1841, made their camp in the central chamber.

The small, plain building at the north end of the palace is the **House of the Turtles** (*Casa de las Tortugas*), named after the turtle sculptures which adorn the cornice. At the south end rises the **Great Pyramid** (*Gran Pirámide*), which has been restored on one side only. The temple at the top has carvings of macaws or parrots. From here you can look down at the unrestored square to the west. All that remains is a decorative masonry crest perforated by small rectangular windows, which has prompted the name **The Dovecote Group** (*Grupo del Palomar*).

The graceful façade of the Palace of the Governor catches the morning light.

85

THE PUUC ROUTE

There are four other, smaller, Mayan ruins in the Puuc region within easy reach of Uxmal. Nearest is **Kabah**, older than Uxmal, and famous for the extraordinary **Codz-Poop**, or **Palace of the Masks**. This rectangular building is 150 ft (46 m) long and its walls are completely covered in Chaac masks.

The Mayan name means 'rolled up sleeping mat', a reference to the rain god's curled up nose. Across the road a path leads among overgrown

A ceremonial archway (below) and intricate carvings (right) grace the ruins at Labriá.

ruins to a restored archway at the beginning of a *sacbe*, a Mayan 'white road' leading off to the south. Remains of such roads have been found all over the Yucatán.

Three miles (5 km) on is **Sayil**, where a grand, three-storey **palace** rises out of the bush. Its colonnaded façades bear carvings of the Descending God which figures prominently at Tulum. Other ruins lie hidden in the bird-haunted woods beyond the palace, including the **Mirador** (look-out), a small temple with a tall, perforated roof crest. A path round to the left of the Mirador leads to a thatched shelter protecting a crude statue of a well-endowed male figure, perhaps some sort of fertility idol.

Another 3 miles (5 km) leads to **Xlapac**, a small archaeological site where you park your car among the caretaker's hens and turkeys. There is only one restored building here, a small Puuc-style structure with stacks of three Chaac masks at the corners and above the central

doorways. Behind the building is a *chultún*, or cistern, which is still used by the caretaker and his family as a storing place for water.

One more 3-mile stint brings you to **Labná**. This large site has another impressive **palace**, similar in style to the one at Kabah. The ornamental stonework is of particular interest, and includes carvings of a human face emerging from a serpent's open jaws.

A *sacbe* leads from the palace towards another group of buildings, dominated by the **Mirador**, a small, crested temple sitting on top of an unrestored pyramid.

Below is the famous **arch** of Labná, which seems to have served as a ceremonial entrance. Here you can clearly see the way in which the Maya constructed their arches and roof vaults – with two masonry walls gradually leaning towards each other, and capped by a course of flat stones. Somehow the Maya never discovered the principle of the keystone, which was used by the ancient **88** Greeks and Romans.

Don't leave this area without paying a visit to the **Caves of Loltún** (*Grutas de Loltún*), a further 11 miles (18 km) beyond Labná. This series of vast limestone caverns was inhabited during neolithic times and was sacred to the Maya, who came here to mine red clay from the cave floor, to collect water from natural basins, and to make offerings to the important gods of the underworld.

Your guide will point out *metates* (grinding stones) left as offerings, Mayan handprints adorning the cave walls, ancient carvings, strangely shaped limestone formations, and two musical stalactites – bang them with your fist and they sing out their name 'Loltún'! The caves can be visited by guided tour only and these tours are run daily at 9.30 and 11.00 a.m., and 12.30, 2.00 and 3.30 p.m.

*S*unlight pours into a cavern at the exit from the impressive Loltún caves.

What to Do

Sports

The warm blue waters of the Caribbean are a paradise for watersports. Divers and snorkellers can enjoy some of the finest coral reefs in the world, while windsurfers will find ideal conditions in the Bahía de Mujeres. There are plenty of activities for landlubbers too, and you can even take to the air in a microlight aircraft or go parasailing high above the waves. Activities can be arranged through your hotel or travel agency, or you can go along to one of the many marinas that line Nichupté Lagoon.

SCUBA DIVING AND SNORKELLING

If you can swim you can snorkel, and it would be a crime to come to Cancún without giving it a try. Snorkelling opens a window into a colourful undersea world teeming with tropical fish. Equipment can be hired at diving shops and beaches. Cancún is the place to learn to dive. Warm shallow water and experienced instructors make it all seem less intimidating, and you can choose between a 'resort dive' crash course, which takes only a couple of hours and qualifies

An instructor gives students a final important briefing before their first dive.

Coral Reefs

A coral reef is one of the great natural wonders of the world. Built up slowly over hundreds of thousands of years by the action of millions of tiny coral polyps and other organisms, a coral reef provides an environment in which countless species of fish, crustacea, molluscs and other invertebrates can flourish.

The coral polyp is a tiny animal, 0.25-1 inch (0.5-3 cm) across, looking something like a sea anemone (to which it is related). The polyps grow in colonies, feeding on animal matter carried to them on the ocean currents, growing, reproducing and depositing new layers of calcium carbonate on, over and around each other. The shape of the colonies varies with the species of coral, the water depth and the action of surf and ocean currents, to give the varieties known as brain coral, staghorn and elkhorn coral, mushroom coral, table coral and star coral. Over the centuries, the continual secretion of new limestone beneath the layers of living coral polyps, bound together with fragments of broken coral and calcareous algae and the remains of sponges and bivalves, builds up great stony coral heads, which eventually merge to form a coral reef.

Coral requires clear, warm, shallow waters, with the average sea temperature staying around 73-77 °F all year round, and a sea bed no deeper than 75 ft (23 m). Sunlight is important, as the coral polyps live in association with photosynthetic algae, which help them to grow. The coral grows very slowly, about 0.25-1 inches (0.5-2.5 cm) a year, so if you break off a piece only 4 inches (10 cm) long, it could take up to 20 years to grow back – snorkellers and divers take heed!

The best known coral reef is the Great Barrier Reef in Australia, which is the largest structure ever built by living creatures, stretching for 1250 miles (2011 km) along the coast of Queensland. The Belize Barrier Reef extends for over 150 miles (241 km) from the Gulf of Honduras to the Banco de Chinchorro off the coast of southern Yucatán – fifth longest in the world.

you for a shallow dive accompanied by the instructor, or you can take a week-long course leading to full certification.

Cozumel's reefs are a major attraction for the experienced diver. All equipment can be hired from the numerous diving shops which line the waterfront at San Miguel, and boat trips normally consist of two dives with a break for lunch on the beach. In case of accidents, an emergency recompression chamber has been installed on the island. Remember that spear fishing, and removing coral, sponges, or objects found on sunken wrecks, are prohibited.

Even if you don't want to be in amongst them, you can admire the reefs from the safety of one of the glass-bottomed boats that go from the Playa Linda Marine Terminal.

SAILING AND WINDSURFING

Cancún's dependable sea breeze makes for good sailing. Hobie cats and Sunfish sail-

boats, and long and short sail-boards can be hired by the hour at marinas and at beaches. Lessons are available. Beginners can learn in safety on the calm waters of Nichupté Lagoon, while experts can hone their skills on the waves in the Bahía de Mujeres.

JET SKIS AND WATER SKIING

The marine equivalent of motorbikes, jet skis are an exciting way to take to the water and can travel at up to 30 mph (50 kph), so beginners should take care until they have mastered the machines.

If you do fall off, the faithful sea-horse will automatically cruise in circles until you get back on. They are very popular in Cancún, and can be hired from most beaches and marinas.

PARASAILING AND ULTRALIGHT FLIGHTS

Parasailing is very popular in Cancún. If you want to give it a go, you'll be securely strapped into a harness, attached to the billowing canopy, and before you can say 'Now wait a minute' you'll be going up like an express lift with your heart in your mouth and your stomach somewhere back on the beach. The line is attached to a boat which will take you for a cruise along the shore, flying

On or above the waves, Cancún offers a wide variety of fun watersports.

93

you like a kite – you don't have to do anything but enjoy the view – before depositing you gently back where you started.

A more sophisticated, though no less exciting way to take to the skies is to try out the passenger seat in an ultralight seaplane, a tiny aircraft like a hang-glider with an engine. The views of the city and coast from the air are fantastic. Flights can be arranged at a couple of marinas on the lagoon.

FISHING

The waters off the Mexican coast offer some of the best big-game fishing in the world: kingfish, dorado, tuna, shark, barracuda and tarpon are there for the taking. Billfish tournaments are held in Cancún, Isla Mujeres and Cozumel when the marlin and sailfish pass through in April-July. Bottom fishing on the banks around the islands can produce handsome catches of grouper, yellowtail and red snapper, all good eating. Skippered sport-fishing boats carrying four or eight anglers can be hired for four, six or eight hours, with tackle, bait and lunch provided. Shop around the marinas for the best prices.

GOLF

Cancún has the Pok-Ta-Pok 18-hole course, at km 6.5 in the Hotel Zone. It is set on a finger of land poking into the lagoon. The club is open daily 6 a.m. to 6 p.m., last tee-off at 4 p.m. The Meliá Cancún and Oasis Hotels both have their own 9-hole courses. A second 18-hole course is planned for the southern end of the Hotel Zone.

TENNIS

The Pok-Ta-Pok Golf Club and most of the big hotels have their own private courts, often floodlit, and there will usually be a coach on hand to offer advice.

HORSE-RIDING

Horses can be hired for guided treks along the beach and through the jungle, at Rancho Loma Bonita and Xcaret Park south of Cancún, and at a number of ranchos on Cozumel.

Folklore and Fiestas

You can hear traditional Mexican songs and music at the fiesta nights which are held regularly in Cancún's major hotels, but a better idea is to try out one of the restaurants downtown.

Many have a *mariachi* band playing inside, or perhaps a lone minstrel with guitar will serenade you. One or two spots boast a *marimba*, a traditional Latin American instrument similar to a xylophone, often played by two players at once. For a fully fledged extravaganza of regional Mexican dance, music, and song, head for the Ballet Folklorico, which shows at the Continental Villas Plaza Hotel. A delicious Mexican meal is included in the entrance fee. If you are lucky enough to be in Mérida on a Sunday, you can enjoy the performances of Yucatecan music and folk dances that are sponsored by City Hall, and even join a staged traditional wedding celebration.

Here are some dates you should note in your diary if you want catch a whole town enjoying itself out in the streets:

Carnaval, or **Mardi Gras** (the week leading up to Ash Wednesday, which falls in February or March) comprises parades and music in the streets of downtown Cancún, Isla Mujeres and San Miguel de Cozumel, with colourfully decorated floats and dancers sambaing fit to bust, and a ceremony to crown the *Reina del Carnaval* (the Carnival Queen).

Festival del Cedral (1-3 May). The annual agricultural show at El Cedral on Cozumel, with music, dancing, games and bullfights.

Cancún Jazz Festival (late May). Sessions by top international jazz musicians. Check with Tourist Information (see p.130) for more details.

Fiesta de San Miguel (last week in September). Cozumel celebrates the feast of its patron saint, accompanied by dancing, music and fireworks.

Fiesta del Señor de Las Ampollas (27 September-14 October). Mérida hosts two **95**

weeks of fireworks, music, street parades and religious processions in the name of 'Christ of the Blisters', the famous scorched crucifix in the city's cathedral.

Fiesta del Cristo de Sitilpech (18-25 October). A religious festival in Izamal, near Mérida, in which an

Local children big and small don colourful costumes for Cancún's carnival parade.

image of Christ is carried by a procession from the village of Sitilpech to the church at Izamal, a few miles away, accompanied by fireworks and dancing.

All Souls' Day (1-2 November). Candlelit vigils in cemeteries and graveside feasts honour the souls of departed relatives, represented by papier-maché skeletons and skull-shaped sweets.

Feast of the Immaculate Conception (3-9 December). Celebrated at Izamal, near Mérida, and Kantunilkin, 50 miles (80 km) west of Cancún, this is a week of colourful religious processions, music, dancing and fireworks.

Shopping

Shopping must rank as the second most popular pastime in Cancún next to sunbathing, and the planners have taken this into account – few beaches are more than 10 minutes' leisurely stroll away from the nearest shopping plaza. To make things even easier, most places will readily accept dollars, and if you find the afternoons too short, you can keep on shopping until 9 or 10 p.m. Apart from silver jewellery, there are few real bargains to be found in Cancún, but what the heck, it's fun just looking!

The big shopping malls, like Plaza Caracol, Plaza Flamingo and Plaza Kukulcán, are marble-floored, air-conditioned temples. Hardened shoppers can wander at will through the labyrinths of designer boutiques, art galleries, craft shops, perfume counters, jewellery arcades and sports stores. The Plaza La Fiesta, along the road from the Caracol, has a very good selection of folk art.

For slightly lower prices head downtown to the Ki-Huic and Pancho Villa Handicrafts Markets or the Plaza Mexico. Here you can browse through a huge selection of Mexican arts and crafts, and haggle to your heart's content. But remember that, with thousands of tourists passing through, crooks and con-men are inevitably attracted, so be on your guard. **97**

Real bargain hunters and veteran hagglers should make for Mérida, where the Mercado Municipal provides a happy hunting ground for hammocks, *guayaberas*, *huipiles*, Panama hats and other local specialities.

The environmentally aware shopper should think twice about buying anything made of black coral or tortoiseshell. Both the coral and the hawksbill turtle are endangered species and your purchase will only help to hasten their demise. It is also against the law to take items made of these materials into the USA or EC. Anyway, there are plenty of other goodies you can choose from. Here are some suggestions:

Basket work (*canasta*). Basket-making has been practised in the Yucatán since pre-Hispanic times. Choose from woven mats, fans and toys as well as bags and baskets.

Beachwear. T-shirts, bikinis and swimsuits in vivid fluorescent colours and attractive designs are very popular.

Blankets (*sarape*). Brightly coloured, striped Mexican blankets and shawls make good, inexpensive souvenirs.

Crafts. Mayan motifs – Chac Mool, feathered serpents, three-legged pots, toucans, jaguars – can be found in onyx, obsidian, silver, gold, copper, ceramics, stoneware, wood, papier mâché…you name it!

Glassware. Intricate, hand-blown glass sculptures, bowls, pitchers, vases and tumblers are widely available.

Guayaberas. Short-sleeved pleated cotton shirts – the traditional garb of Yucatecan men.

Snack-bar, Mexican-style – tropical fruit to refresh the weary shopper on Isla Mujeres.

Hammocks (*hamacas*). A traditional product of the Yucatán, *hamacas* come in three sizes – single (*sencillo*), double (*doble*), and family size (*matrimonial*), and should be tightly woven from good-quality cotton. Mérida has the best selection.

Hats. *Sombreros* in straw or leather, plain or elaborately decorated, and top-quality Panama hats.

Huaraches. Traditional hand-tooled leather sandals.

Huipiles. The traditional dress worn by Mayan women, a simple white cotton slip with colourful embroidery.

Leather (*cuero*). Good-quality luggage, handbags, belts, boots, saddles, rifle cases, boots and bags in snakeskin and crocodile.

Alcoholic drinks. Take home a taste of Mexico with a bottle of *tequila*, *mezcal*, *Kahlúa*, or *xtabentún* (a delicious Mayan concoction of honey and anise).

Masks (*mascara*). Hand-painted wooden ceremonial masks from Oaxaca, Guerrero and Michoacan are everywhere.

Cheap and cheerful – colourful bargains tempt the souvenir hunter at crafts markets. **99**

Silver (*plata*). Mexico is the world's leading producer of silver, and the prices here are competitive. Always check that items sold as silver bear a '925' stamp, the guarantee of 92.5% purity. If not, it is probably a cheap alloy called *alpaca* or 'nickel silver'.

Nightlife

There's no excuse for an early night in Cancún, unless by early you mean early in the morning. The bars and nightclubs sizzle through the night, and it's not unusual for serious party animals to see the sun rise as they head back to their hotel. All tastes are catered for in this cosmopolitan resort, from an evening's traditional Mexican music to ear-splitting heavy rock; from cool jazz to stand-up comedy.

The major hotels all have lively lobby bars, and many stage their own entertainment in the evenings, but the adventurous will want to go club crawling. Many bars and clubs are concentrated around the busy Plaza Caracol area, and along the Paseo Kukulcán downtown.

Ask a waiter or your hotel receptionist where the current hot spots are. Carlos'n'Charlie's, Guadalajara Grill and the Hard Rock Café are lively restaurant-bars with a good party atmosphere. Later in the evening you might want to check out the more sophisticated nightclubs like Dady'O, Christine's and La Boom, all of which play the latest music, and have spectacular laser shows. For reggae, try Jalapenos, or head downtown to Cat's, on Avenida Yaxchilán.

If you are a fan of stand-up comedy, the Fiesta Americana Condesa Hotel offers top American comics six nights a week (not Sundays). On Saturdays you can join the locals in the Parque de Palapas for open-air gigs by local bands – this could mean rock, funk, jazz, salsa, folk.

Or leave the land behind and take a party cruise to Isla Mujeres. Several marinas offer evening trips across the bay for a moonlit party on the beach, with barbecue, drinks, party games and on-board disco.

Cozumel also has no shortage of lively clubs. When the cruise ships are in harbour, the little town of San Miguel really comes alive. Try Scaramouche or Neptuno's, or join the queues to get into the offshore branch of Carlos'n'Charlie's. If you find that dancing isn't energetic enough for you, there's a volleyball court at the back of the bar!

If nightclubs aren't your idea of a good night out, shopping continues well after sunset at Cancún's plush Plaza Caracol.

Eating Out

As befits a major international resort, Cancún boasts a range of restaurants to suit all tastes and pockets. You can eat German or Japanese, Italian or Arabic, Mexican or Mayan. You can snack at a simple sidewalk café, dine *à la haute cuisine* in a sophisticated hotel restaurant, or enjoy fresh Caribbean seafood on an evening cruise to Isla Mujeres. And if you find yourself hankering for a hamburger, all your favourite fast-food chains can be found here too.

MEAL TIMES

Breakfast (*el desayuno*) is generally served from 7 a.m. to 11 a.m., and dinner (*la cena*) from 7 p.m. to 10.30 p.m., while lunch (*la comida*), the main meal of the day, is a movable feast eaten any time between noon and 4 p.m. In fact, in Cancún's easy-going atmosphere, any time is meal time. Many restaurants are open all day (a few are open 24 hours), and you can easily find a place to eat any time between 7 a.m. and midnight. Many restaurants offer a good-value set-price lunch (*comida corrida*).

BREAKFAST

All hotels and most restaurants offer a choice of American, Continental or Mexican-style breakfasts. Start the day simply with a light meal of *café con leche* (coffee with milk) and *pan tostado* (toast), or go the whole hog with orange juice, fresh tropical fruit, hotcakes, hash browns, bacon and eggs. If you think you can face it first thing in the morning, try the local *huevos motuleños* – tortillas and refried beans topped with fried eggs and peas, smothered in a sauce of tomatoes, onions and chilli. Guaranteed to start the heart after a night on the tequila!

MEXICAN COOKING

Mexican cuisine is the result of blending the indigenous Aztec and Mayan culinary traditions with the Spanish and Middle

Eastern influences introduced by the conquistadores, and allowing the mixture to simmer for 400 years. You will find that the finished dish is a rich and varied cuisine, far more exotic and exciting than you might expect, especially if you arrive with preconceptions based on experiences of Tex-Mex restaurants back home.

In Mexico you will meet the flavours of coriander and cumin, chillies and bitter chocolate, tart, tangy limes and smooth, rich avocado.

But first, the basics. The staples of the Mexican kitchen are the same today as they were thousands of years ago when the native Indians first began to till the soil – corn, beans and chillies.

Corn (*maís*) can be eaten on the cob (when it is known as *elote*), but is principally used as cornmeal for making tortillas, the round pancakes that accompany almost every Mexican meal. The dried corn is boiled with lime to loosen the tough skin, then the cooked kernels are dried and ground into flour. The flour is mixed with a little water to make a firm dough, and patted out by expert hands into thin pancakes about 15 cm (6 in) in diameter (these days, a tortilla press does the job more quickly and efficiently, but you may still see women making tortillas by hand at market stalls and in tourist restaurants). The tortillas are cooked on a griddle, and served as an accompaniment, or as an integral part of the meal.

There are countless variations on the tortilla theme. *Tacos* are tortillas rolled around a filling of shredded, barbecued pork, beef or chicken, and vegetables, perhaps deep-fried. *Enchiladas* are stuffed tortillas smothered in sauce and baked. *Tostadas* are crisp, fried tortillas, topped with meat or fish and various sauces (*tostaditas* are quartered tortillas, deep-fried, served with salsa and guacamole – you may know them as 'tortilla chips'). *Chilaquiles* are fried tortilla strips and meat filling layered in a casserole and baked. *Quesadillas* are tortillas topped with grilled cheese and ham and served with refried beans. **103**

Some Yucatecan variations are *panuchos*, tortillas stuffed with black-bean paste, fried and topped with chicken, onion and tomato; and *papadzules*, tortillas stuffed with hard-boiled egg, with a sauce of tomato and onion spiked with chilli and ground pumpkin seeds.

Beans (*frijoles*) are usually red kidney beans, and turn up in soups and stews. But you will come across them most often in the form of *frijoles refritos* (refried beans), a tasty accompaniment to most traditional Mexican dishes. Refried beans are made by boiling red kidney beans or black beans until they are tender, then mashing them into a paste in a frying pan with sautéed onion, garlic and chilli.

Perhaps the ingredient most people think of when they think of Mexican cooking is the **chilli pepper**. However, you would be wrong if you thought that all Mexican food is stoked to a fiery heat with red-hot chillies – or indeed that all peppers are

*E*njoy a lively meal down-town with music from the Three Amigos...

themselves hot. Peppers have been cultivated in Mexico since prehistoric times, and today there are estimated to be between 60 and 100 different varieties throughout the world, from the large, sweet, red and green bell peppers you can buy in your local supermarket, to the tiny, excruciatingly hot *prik khii nuu* chillies from Thailand. Among the more common varieties you will experience in Mexico are the large, red and wrinkly *ancho*, with a rich, mild flavour, and the hotter *serrano*, which is smooth, green and tapered. *Jalapeño* peppers are longer, thinner and hotter than *serranos*, while the local Yucatecan

*O*r alternatively, sip an un-hurried beer on the beach with just the birds for company.

pepper is the *habanero*, which is lantern-shaped, about 1½ in (4 cm) long, and can be green, yellow or red depending on how ripe it is. *Habaneros* have a rich, distinctive flavour and are fiery hot. The one to watch out for is the *chipotle* pepper, a dark red, wrinkly dried pepper used in the hottest of sauces.

No Mexican feast will be complete without a stack of warm tortillas and a dish or two of cold sauces. *Salsa cruda* displays Mexico's national colours of red, white **105** and green in a blend of chopped tomato, onion, chilli and fresh coriander, while *guacamole* is a delicious blend of finely chopped avocado, tomato, onion, garlic, chilli and coriander. A local speciality is *Ixni-Pec*, a very hot sauce made with *habanero* chillies, onion, tomato and sour-orange juice – use with caution!

CLASSIC MEXICAN DISHES

Perhaps the most famous of all Mexican dishes is *mole poblano de Guajolote*, a stew of wild turkey in a richly flavoured sauce of tomatoes, chillies, garlic, nuts, spices, and chocolate, which is reputed to have been served in the palace of Moctezuma, the Aztec emperor.

Another national classic is *pescado a la Veracruzana*, or fish Veracruz-style. The fish is traditionally red snapper (*huachinango*), or grouper (*mero*) and is prepared surrounded by a fragrant sauce of tomatoes, onions, capers and olives, scented with cinnamon .

*D*elightfully informal, watch your food being cooked, as often as not.

The indigenous cuisine of the Yucatán peninsula (advertised as *cocina tipica*), draws on traditional Mayan recipes. Much use is made of local ingredients such as sour oranges, *achiote* (the ground seeds of the annatto tree), limes, *cilantro* (fresh coriander), and *habanero* chillies.

Classic Yucatecan dishes are *sopa de lima* (a hearty soup of chicken, vegetables and crisp-fried tortilla strips, flavoured with lime juice); *poc chuc* (pork marinated in a paste of *achiote*, cumin seeds, garlic, and peppercorns, served with sour-orange sauce); *pollo ticuleño* (breaded chicken fillet in tomato sauce, served with tortillas, beans, and garnished with radish flowers, sliced bananas and peas); *pollo píbil* (chicken marinated in *achiote* paste and sour-orange sauce, and baked in banana leaves).

Don't miss the chance to sample the succulent Caribbean seafood. *Langosta* (lobster) and *camarón* (prawns) are delicious simply grilled, or fried and served with garlic sauce. Conch (an abalone-like shellfish), shrimp and white fish, marinated with lime juice, and seasoned with raw tomato, onion, chilli and coriander, make the popular appetizer called *ceviche*.

DESSERTS

The usual way to round off dinner is with a platter of fresh, tropical fruits: sweet, juicy pineapple, refreshing papaya and melon, succulent mango and banana, or tangy orange. For something more filling, try *arroz con leche* (rice pudding with raisins), or *flan* (crème caramel).

Some restaurants offer famous 'Flaming Desserts': the house lights are dimmed while the waiter makes a spectacular pyrotechnic show of pouring burning brandy or tequila in a flickering bluecascade over some confection of cake, fruit or ice-cream.

DRINKS

Mexican beer (*cerveza*) is excellent, and is exported all **107** over the world. It comes in two varieties, light (*clara*) and dark (*negra*), and has a higher alcoholic content than most North American beers.

Labels to look out for include Bohemia, Dos Equis, Sol and Corona. Imported wines are available in the better restaurants, but Mexican wine, from the vineyards of Baja California in the north west of the country, is well worth trying.

The national tipple is tequila, a fiery spirit distilled from the fermented juice of the agave plant. It is traditionally knocked back neat, accompanied by a pinch of salt and a twist of lime, or sipped slowly in a Margarita, a cocktail of tequila, triple sec, lime juice and crushed ice, served in a salt-rimmed glass.

Another popular cocktail is the Tequila Sunrise, a colourful concoction of tequila, crème de cassis, lime juice and grenadine. *Mezcal* is a regional variation of tequila distinguished by the presence of a pickled *agave* worm at the bottom of the bottle – not for the squeamish – and Mexican brandy (*conac*) is very popular with the locals.

Kahlúa is a pleasant coffee-flavoured Mexican liqueur, but a more exotic after-dinner drink is *xtabentún*, a Mayan liqueur flavoured with fermented honey and *anise*.

Familiar brands of soft drinks (*refrescos*) are bottled under licence in Mexico, and are available everywhere, as are Mexican, Canadian and European mineral waters. A delicious alternative to carbonated drinks are freshly prepared tropical fruit juices and shakes – look for a sign saying *Jugos y Licuados*.

Coffee is usually served black – if you want it with milk ask for *café con leche*. A spicy Mexican variation is *café de olla*, which is coffee brewed in a small earthenware pot (*olla*) with cinnamon, cloves and brown sugar. Camomile tea (*té de manzanilla*) is a refreshing change from coffee, and is known to be particularly good for settling an upset stomach.

BLUEPRINT
for a
Perfect Trip

UNITED STATES OF AMERICA

BAJA CALIFORNIA NORTE

SONORA

CHIHUAHUA

COAHUILA

BAJA CALIFORNIA SUR

DURANGO

NUEVO LEÓN

GULF OF MEXICO

SINALOA

ZACATECAS

NAYARIT

SAN LUIS POTOSÍ

TAMAU-LIPAS

QUERÉTARO

HIDALGO

Cancún

YUCATAN

Mérida

Cozumel

AGUASCALIENTES

GUANAJUATO

JALISCOS

TLAXCALA

PUEBLA

CAMPECHE

QUINTANA ROO

COLIMA

MICHOACÁN

VERACRUZ

TABASCO

MÉXICO STATE

DISTRITO FEDERAL

GUERRERO

OAXACA

CHIAPAS

BELIZE

MORELOS

HONDURAS

GUATEMALA

EL SALVADOR

PACIFIC OCEAN

An A–Z Summary of Practical Information and Facts

A

ACCOMMODATION (*alojamiento*)

(See also CAMPING and YOUTH HOSTELS).

Luxury hotels line the beach in **Cancún**'s Hotel Zone, and building is still going on – a total of about 150 hotels by 1995 is planned. The architecture ranges from Mediterranean-style villas to stunning glass pyramids and huge thatched *palapas*, with every imaginable variation on the theme of the Mayan temple pyramid. All rooms have bathroom, air conditioning and satellite television, with views of either ocean or lagoon. More moderately priced hotels are to be found in downtown Cancún, a brief bus or taxi ride from the beaches. Advance reservations are strongly recommended during the high season (December–April): if you arrive without a reservation, the accommodation desk at the airport should be able to find you a room. Condominiums and furnished suites are sprouting all over the island, and offer good value self-catering accommodation. Hotel prices can drop by as much as half during the low season (May–December).

Cozumel has a few luxury hotels, but most of the accommodation here is in the middle- to low-budget range. The cheaper hotels are in San Miguel, with the more expensive ones stretching for a few miles along the coast to north and south.

I'd like a single/double room with bath/shower.	**Quisiera una habitación sencilla/doble con baño/regadera.**
What's the rate per night?	**¿Cuál es el precio por noche?**
Where is there a cheap hotel?	**¿Dónde hay un hotel económico?**

AIRPORTS *(aeropuertos)*

Cancún's International Airport lies 12 miles (20 km) south of the city, and handles both international and domestic flights. Hotel reservations desks, a currency exchange counter, car rental agencies, duty-free shops, restaurant and bars are all available. Your hotel may provide a courtesy bus or limousine service, otherwise transport to the Hotel Zone and downtown Cancún is provided by the airport minibus service (buy your ticket from the booth beside the exit from the terminal building, departures every 30 minutes), or by taxi. The minibus service runs one way only, so you will need to take a taxi to return to the airport (unless, of course, your hotel provides transport). An airport tax of US$12 (or the equivalent in pesos) per person is levied on departing international flights, and US$4 for domestic flights.

Cozumel's small international airport lies on the northern edge of San Miguel, and has an information desk, car rental agencies, shops, bar and restaurant. Taxis and minibuses provide transport to hotels and downtown San Miguel.

Porter!	**Maletero!**
Where's the bus for ...?	**¿Dónde está el camión para...?**

B

BICYCLE and SCOOTER HIRE *(renta de bicicletas y motocicletas)*

Bicycles, mopeds and scooters can be hired in Cancún, on Isla Mujeres and on Cozumel, where they are a cheap and convenient form of transport. A cash deposit (credit card for mopeds and scooters) will be required as security. Make sure the bike is in full working order and is adjusted for comfortable riding before you accept it. Mexican law makes wearing a crash helmet compulsory while riding a moped or scooter, but the law is not always enforced. **111**

CAMPING (*campismo*)

Camping is available at the CREA Youth Hostel in the Hotel Zone, with use of the hostel facilities. On **Isla Mujeres**, you can camp rough anywhere on the island's beaches, but there are no facilities. On **Cozumel** you will require a camping permit (*permiso de acampar*), available from the Naval Base (free). Again, camping is rough, with no water or facilities laid on. For further information on camping in the Yucatán, contact Agencia Nacional de Turismo Juvenil (see YOUTH HOSTELS), for hostel-affiliated sites.

May we camp here?	**¿Podemos acampar aquí?**
We have a tent/trailer.	**Tenemos una tienda de caravana/campaña/una**

CAR HIRE (*renta de autos*)

There are dozens of car rental agencies in Cancún, both international and local. However, whether you decide on a jeep, a saloon, or the ubiquitous Volkswagen Beetle, renting a car in Cancún is not cheap. Expect to pay at least US$55 a day, including tax, insurance, collision damage waiver and unlimited mileage. Weekly rates may be slightly more favourable. You will need a valid driving licence and a major credit card, and must be over 18 years of age (21 or 25 at certain agencies). Check the car thoroughly before leaving to make sure that everything is in working order, and that any dents or scratches have been recorded on the rental agreement.

Avis: Mayfair Plaza, Hotel Zone; tel. 83-00-04.
Budget: Av. Tulum 214, Cancún City; tel. 84-02-04.
Hertz: c/Reno 35, Cancún City; tel. 84-13-26.

I'd like to rent a car for today/	**Quisiera rentar un coche para hoy/**
tomorrow.	**mañana.**
for one day/one week	**por un día/una semana**

CLIMATE

The Yucatán peninsula enjoys a tropical climate, hot and humid throughout the year. The dry season extends from December to May, which is the peak period for tourism. There are, on average, 234 clear days a year, concentrated within the dry season. Daytime temperatures rarely slip below 80 °F (27 °C), peaking around 90 °F in April and May. Occasionally a short-lived rainstorm is heralded by a cooler wind from the north (known as *el norte*). During the wet season, from mid May to October, expect daily rainfall and increased humidity, but little escape from the heat. The hurricane season is July–October, and of about ten hurricanes that form in the Atlantic each year, two or three might touch the Yucatán coast. The worst of these in recent years was Hurricane Gilbert in 1988, whose effects are still evident in some places along the coast.

	J	F	M	A	M	J	J	A	S	O	N	D
°C	21	21	22	24	26	27	28	29	27	26	23	21
°F	69	70	71	74	78	81	82	84	81	78	73	70

CLOTHING

Think cool and casual – lightweight cotton shirts, shorts and skirts are best for Cancún's relentless heat. Don't forget sun-hat and sun-glasses for protection from the strong tropical sunshine. Bring your own beachwear or buy it from the dozens of shops piled high with the fluorescent shorts and T-shirts which form acceptable attire from seaside to shopping mall. You might like to wear something slightly smarter in the evenings, for visiting restaurants or touring the nightclubs, but bright and informal is still the rule – jacket and tie are rarely seen. A light sweater may be useful on cool, clear evenings. Those venturing away from Cancún should dress a little more formally, especially if you intend to visit any churches. You'll need a pair of comfortable walking shoes or boots, a sun-hat, and some insect repellent for exploring the archaeological sites.

COMPLAINTS

Any complaints should be taken up with the management of the hotel, restaurant or shop involved. If you do not obtain satisfaction, you should take your grievance to the Secretaríat of Tourism (SEC-TUR) Office (see TOURIST INFORMATION on p.130).

CRIME

You should take the usual precautions against theft – don't carry large amounts of cash, leave your valuables in the hotel safe, not in your room, and beware of pickpockets in crowded areas. Never leave your bags or valuables on view in a parked car – take them with you or lock them in the boot. Any theft or loss must be reported immediately to the police in order to comply with your travel insurance. If your passport is lost or stolen, you should also inform your consulate.

I want to report a theft.   **Quiero denunciar un robo.**

CUSTOMS (*aduana*) and ENTRY FORMALITIES

Entry procedures are fast and straightforward. Visitors must have a passport and a tourist card, issued at border crossings and by Mexican embassies, travel agents, and airlines serving Mexico. This card is free and valid for three months, and is renewable for a further three months on application to an immigration office, though the renewal process is very time consuming. It will be stamped on entry and must be kept with you for presentation on departure. If you lose it, report the loss to the local immigration office to avoid long delays on departure.

The following chart shows what main duty-free items you may take into Mexico and, when returning home, to your own country:

Into:	Cigarettes		Cigars		Tobacco	Spirits		Wine
Mexico	400	or	50	or	250 g	3 l	or	3 l
Australia	250	or	200	or	250 g	1.1 l	or	1.1 l
Canada	200	or	50	and	1 kg	1.1 l	or	1.1 l

Into:	Cigarettes		Cigars		Tobacco	Spirits		Wine
Eire	200	or	50	or	250 g	1 l	or	2 l
N Zealand	200	or	50	or	250 g	1.1 l	and	4.5 l
S Africa	400	and	50	and	250 g	1 l	and	2 l
UK	200	or	50	or	250 g	1 l	and	2 l
USA	200	and	100	and	*	1 l	and	1 l
* A reasonable quantity								

Currency restrictions. Non-residents may import or export any amount of freely convertible foreign currency into Mexico, provided that it is declared on arrival. There is no limit to the amount of Mexican currency you may carry into or out of Mexico.

I have nothing to declare.   **No tengo nada que declarar.**

D

DISABLED TRAVELLERS

Special facilities for disabled travellers are restricted to Cancún's luxury hotels and the newer shopping malls. Downtown Cancún is more difficult to cope with, and public transport is not accessible. Although there are no special provisions, most of the archaeological site at Chichén Itzá can be negotiated by wheelchair.

DRIVING

A current US, Canadian or British driving licence is acceptable in Mexico. If you are planning to bring your own car, note that new requirements for the temporary entry of vehicles from the USA were instituted 8 January, 1992. Owners must: a) provide documentary evidence that the vehicle carries full US auto insurance (theft, third party and comprehensive) valid for at least two months; b) post a bond based on the value of the vehicle as determined by Mexican **115** customs officials at time of entry (could be as high as 50%). This bond will be reimbursed on departure, but a processing fee will be charged. For further information, contact your nearest Mexican Embassy. The US Department of State issues a pamphlet – *Tips for Travellers to Mexico* – available for $1.00 from Superintendent of Documents, US Government Printing Office, Washington DC 20401.

Driving conditions. In Cancún, main intersections are controlled by traffic lights (*semaforos*), or roundabouts (*glorietas*). At a *glorieta*, you must give way to vehicles already in the roundabout, i.e. coming from the left. Pedestrian crossings on Avenida Tulum downtown are marked by paved humps in the road – give way to pedestrians.

Areas where you are not allowed to park are marked by a sign with the letter E with a line through, or by a red-painted kerb. A white-painted kerb means parking is legal at all times, yellow during off-peak hours only.

Speed limits in towns are 30 or 40 kph, 60 kph in the Hotel Zone, 80 kph on most highways, and 110 kph on the dual carriageway south of Cancún. Watch out for speed bumps (*topes*) in built-up areas and when approaching towns and villages – you will have to slow to a crawl to cross them without damaging your car.

Petrol. Sales of petrol (*gasolina*) are monopolized by the government petroleum company Pemex. Grades are regular (*nova*), super (*extra*), and lead-free (*Magna Sin*), sold by the litre. Note that Pemex does not accept credit cards. Keep your eye on the fuel gauge as distances between petrol stations can be long.

Road signs. Most Mexican road signs are the standard international pictographs, but you will also encounter these written signs:

Alto	Stop
Ceda el paso	Give way
Circulacion	Direction of traffic
Cruce de peatones	Pedestrian crossing
Curva peligrosa	Dangerous bend
Cuidado	Caution
Cuota	Toll
Desviacion	Detour

Disminuya su velocidad	Reduce speed
Escuela	School
Peligro	Danger
Prohibido estacionarse	No parking
Prohibido rebasar	No overtaking
Salida de camiones	Truck exit

Breakdown. In case of breakdown, get your vehicle off the road if possible. The main highways are patrolled twice a day between 8 a.m. and 8 p.m. by the Green Angels (*Angeles Verdes*), a government-sponsored highway patrol that provides a free breakdown and information service for tourists. If you can reach a telephone, call their 24-hour hotline on 250-8417.

(International) driver's licence	**Licencia para manejar (internacional)**
Car registration papers	**registro del automóvil**
Are we on the right road for ...?	**¿Es ésta la carretera hacia ...?**
Fill the tank, top grade, please.	**Llénelo, por favor, con super.**
Check the oil/tyres/battery.	**Revise el aceite/las llantas/la batería.**
I've broken down.	**Mi carro se ha descompuesto.**
There's been an accident.	**Ha habido un accidente.**
Could you mend this puncture?	**¿Puede arreglar este pinchazo?**

E

ELECTRIC CURRENT
Mexico uses the same 120 V/60 Hz system as the USA and Canada.

EMBASSIES and CONSULATES (*embajadas y consuladas*)
British Consulate: Calle 53, no. 498 (corner of Calle 58) Mérida; tel. (99) 216799.

Canadian Consulate: Plaza Mexico, Av. Tulum 200, downtown; tel. 843716.

EMERGENCIES (*emergencias*)

Unless you are fluent in Spanish, you should seek help through your hotel receptionist or the local tourist office. If you can speak Spanish, the following telephone numbers may be useful:

	Cancún	Cozumel
Fire Station (*bomberos*)	841202	20800
Red Cross (*Cruz Roja*)	841616	21058
Police (*policía*)	841913	20092

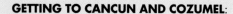

GETTING TO CANCUN AND COZUMEL:

From Great Britain

BY AIR: scheduled flights from London to Cancún, via the USA, are available daily. For details of discounted fares, contact one of the many travel agencies that specialize in flights to Mexico and Latin America. Flight time from London to Cancún (via Houston, for example) is typically around 14 hours, including changeover. Note that travellers flying via the USA will have to clear customs when they change aircraft in America, and British citizens are recommended to obtain a US visa before making their trip.

Charter flights from the UK to Cancún are increasing in number as Mexico promotes Cancún as its European gateway. Contact a travel agent for the latest details of charters and package tours.

From the USA

BY AIR: a number of American and Mexican airlines offer several non-stop, scheduled flights daily between major US cities and

Cancún and Cozumel. Typical flight times are two hours from

Houston or Miami, three and a half hours from Chicago, four hours from New York and five hours from Los Angeles. The least expensive way to fly to Cancún is to take one of the many package deals on offer, which include a return flight, accommodation, and perhaps car rental, all at a very competitive price. Check with a travel agent for details.

BY ROAD: driving to the Yucatán is only for the adventurous traveller with plenty of time to spare. Although the highways are in good repair, the distance from the Mexican border to Cancún is over 1600 miles, and will take four or five days. It is possible to make the journey from the US down to the Yucatán by bus, but it is a marathon trip with numerous bus changes, and will only be of interest to budget travellers who want to see the rest of Mexico too.

BY RAIL: There are sleeper services from the border towns of Nuevo Laredo, Ciudad Juárez, and Nogales to Mexico City, where you can catch another sleeper to Mérida, a six-hour bus trip from Cancún. Total journey time is three to four days.

GUIDES (guía)

Official guides fluent in English, French or German are on hand, for a fee, at the principal archaeological sites, and their detailed knowledge can greatly increase your enjoyment of the site. It is customary to tip these guides. You can hire a qualified guide independently through the Secretaríat of Tourism (see TOURIST INFORMATION on p.130). Cancún's numerous travel agencies offer a wide range of guided tours to all the main attractions in the area. Ask at your hotel or travel agent for details.

We'd like an English-. speaking guide.	**Queremos un guía que hable inglés.**
I need an English interpreter.	**Necesito un intérprete de inglés.**

LANGUAGE

The official language of Mexico is Spanish. Latin American Spanish differs slightly from the Castilian Spanish of Spain, most noticeably in the pronunciation of soft 'c' and 'z', which are not lisped but have a straightforward 's' sound. About 10% of the Mexican population still speak the indigenous Indian languages. Many of them live in the Yucatán where the Mayan language is still much used in country areas. English is widely understood in tourist areas, especially in Cancún and Cozumel, where you can easily get by without a word of Spanish, but it is polite to learn at least the basic words for hello, goodbye, please and thank you. Mexicans will welcome and encourage any attempt you make to use their language.

The Berlitz phrase book, LATIN-AMERICAN SPANISH FOR TRAVELLERS, covers most situations you are likely to encounter in your visit to Mexico; also useful is the Berlitz English-Spanish pocket dictionary, containing a special menu-reader supplement. (See also USEFUL EXPRESSIONS on the cover of this guide.)

Good morning/good day	**Buenos días**
Good afternoon/evening	**Buenas tardes**
Good night	**Buenas noches**
Goodbye	**Adíos**
See you later	**Hasta luego**
Please	**Por favor**
Thank you	**Gracias**

LOST PROPERTY (*objetos perdidos*)

Ask for advice from your hotel reception or the Tourist Information Office before contacting the police. For items left behind on public transport, ask your hotel receptionist to telephone the bus station or taxi company.

I've lost my wallet/purse/passport.	**He perdido mi cartera/ bolsa/pasaporte.**

MEDICAL CARE

See also EMERGENCIES on p.118. Make sure you take out adequate medical insurance before leaving for Mexico. Vaccinations are not required for visitors to the northern Yucatán, but if your itinerary will take you to the low-lying tropical areas in the south of Mexico, you should seek advice on immunization.

The main health hazard in the Yucatán is also one of its biggest attractions – the sun. Take along a sun-hat, sun-glasses, and plenty of high-factor sunscreen, and limit your sunbathing sessions to an hour or less until you begin to tan. Sunburn can seriously ruin your holiday.

You've probably heard of 'Montezuma's Revenge' (known locally as *turista*), an attack of stomach cramps and diarrhoea caused by contaminated water or food. You can minimize your chances of being laid low by this unpleasant complaint by always washing your hands before eating, avoiding salads, unpeeled fruit, food sold by street vendors, and tap water (don't even brush your teeth with it) – most hotels will provide purified drinking water (*agua purificada*) and ice.

Coffee, tea and bottled drinks are quite safe. If you do get sick, stay in bed, take plenty of fluids with a little salt and sugar, and try to eat small amounts of bland food like dry toast. Avoid spicy foods and alcohol.

Diarrhoea remedies and other medicines can be obtained from the local drugstores (*farmacias*). Information on farmacias that remain open on evenings and holidays will be displayed in the window. In an emergency your hotel will be able to call on an English-speaking doctor. There are English-speaking staff at the Hospital Americano, Calle Viento, downtown Cancún; tel. (988) 846133.

MONEY MATTERS

Currency (*moneda*). The unit of currency in Mexico is the *peso*, denoted by a dollar sign '$', or by the abbreviation ' m.n.' (*moneda* **121**

nacional). Coins in current circulation come in denominations of 50 (now rare), 100, 500, 1000 and 5000 pesos, bills in 2000, 5000, 10,000, 20,000, 50,000 and 100,000 pesos. US dollar bills are also accepted at many tourist shops and restaurants in both Cancún and Cozumel.

Banks and currency exchange offices (*banco; casa de cambio*). Banks are generally open 9 a.m.-1.30 p.m. or 2 p.m. Monday-Friday. Some are also open 3 p.m.-5 p.m., but international currency exchange is usually restricted to between 10 a.m. and 1 p.m. *Casas de cambio* work longer hours, are open weekends, and usually offer slightly better rates. You can also change money at your hotel, but the rate will be less favourable than at a bank.

Traveller's cheques and credit cards (*cheque de viaje; tarjeta de crédito*).

The safest and most convenient way of taking money with you is as US dollar traveller's cheques. They are easily exchanged for cash – take along your passport for identification – and are accepted as cash in most hotels and better restaurants in tourist areas. Major credit cards are widely accepted in hotels, restaurants and tourist-related businesses, but it is wise to ask first. Petrol stations deal in cash only.

I want to change some dollars/pounds.	**Quiero cambiar dólares/libras/esterlinas.**
Do you accept traveller's cheques?	**¿Acepta usted cheques de viajero?**
Can I pay with this credit card?	**¿Puedo pagar con esta arjeta de crédito?**
How much?	**¿Cuánto es?**
Have you anything cheaper?	**¿Tiene algo más barato?**

NEWSPAPERS and MAGAZINES *(periodicos y revistas)*

The News is Mexico's daily English-language newspaper, published in Mexico City, covering Latin American and world current affairs. It is available from newsagents and street news stands in tourist areas. You can also buy *USA Today* and *The Miami Herald*, and a selection of English-language magazines and books (although these are expensive).

Have you any English-language newspapers/magazines?	**¿Tiene periódicos/revistas en inglés?**

OPENING HOURS

Archaeological sites are open daily 8 a.m.-5 p.m., while the Regional Anthropology Museum in Mérida is open 8 a.m.-8 p.m., but is closed Monday. Cozumel Museum opens 10 a.m.-6 p.m., and is closed Saturday.

Banks are open Monday-Friday, 9 a.m.-1.30 p.m. and 3 p.m.-5 p.m., but will deal with currency exchange only in the mornings. Exchange booths keep longer hours, usually 9 a.m.-9 p.m. daily.

Shops normally open 9 or 10 a.m.-9 p.m. Some shops, especially downtown, may close for siesta from around 1 p.m. to 5 p.m.

The **post office** is open 8 a.m.-7 p.m. Monday-Friday, and 9 a.m.-noon on Saturday, closed Sunday.

PHOTOGRAPHY

Major brands of film are widely available in all varieties. In Cancún, Cozumel and Mérida there are laboratories that will process colour print films in a few hours and E-6 slide films by the following day. Cassettes for video cameras are also stocked. At archaeological sites the use of flash or a tripod is not allowed without first obtaining written permission, and the use of a video camera usually entails an additional fee. Beware of the effects of heat on photographic film – never leave your camera or film in direct sunlight. If you are planning to go snorkelling, you may like to try photographing the colourful marine life. Many of the equipment rental shops on the beach hire out waterproof cameras – for best results use 400 ASA colour print film, and make sure your subject is no more than 6 ft (2 m) from the camera.

I'd like a film for this camera.	**Quisiera un rollo para esta cámara.**
a film for colour pictures	**un rollo en color**
for black-and-white	**en blanco y negro**
for colour-slides	**de transparencias**
35-mm-film	**de treinta y cinco**
super-8	**super ocho**
How long will it take to develop (and print) this film?	**¿Cuánto tardará en revelar (y sacar copias de) este rollo?**
May I take a picture?	**¿Puedo tomar una foto?**

PLANNING YOUR BUDGET

To give you an idea of what to expect, here are some average prices in US dollars. These can only be regarded as approximate, as inflation continues to push prices up.

Airport transfer. Minibus from Cancún International Airport to downtown or Hotel Zone $6. Taxi from downtown to airport $12.

Bicycle and moped hire. Bicycles $5-8 a day, plus deposit. Scooters and mopeds $20-40 a day; driving licence and credit card needed.

Buses. Between downtown Cancún and Hotel Zone $0.66. From downtown to Puerto Juárez $0.50. From Cancún to Playa del Carmen $2.66. From Cancún to Mérida $7.

Camping. $1.66-$3.33 per person per night, depending on location and facilities.

Boat and jet ski hire. Jet ski $25 for half an hour. Hobie Cat or Sunfish sailboats $20 an hour. Motor boat $50 an hour.

Car hire. Volkswagen Beetle with unlimited mileage, including tax and collision damage waiver $55 a day, $370 a week.

Entertainment. Cinema $1.33, bullfight $27, nightclub cover charge $7-10, Ballet Folklorico $37 including dinner.

Excursions. Day trip to Isla Mujeres including lunch and snorkelling $40. Overnight coach trip to Chichén Itzá including hotel, meals, guide, Light and Sound Show $100 (day trip $33). Three-day, two-night coach trip to Mérida, Uxmal and other nearby archaeological sites, including hotels, meals and guides $240.

Hotels (double room with bath, high season, Cancún). Deluxe from $150, moderate $70-150, budget $35-70. Prices drop considerably in the low season and away from Cancún.

Ferries (one way). Puerto Juárez to Isla Mujeres $1.50. Playa del Carmen to Cozumel $8.33.

Meals and drinks. Full breakfast $5-8, dinner from $10, coffee $1.00-1.80, glass of orange juice $2, bottle of beer $1.00-2.50, purified water (1 litre) $1.00.

Scuba diving and snorkelling. For qualified divers, two dives (including hire of all equipment) $65. For beginners, four-day course of instruction, including equipment hire, $350. Hire of snorkelling equipment $5. Snorkelling boat trip $10-20.

Sports. Windsurfing $10-12 an hour. Water-skiing $60 an hour. Parascending $40. Microlight flights $45 per person. Golf green fees $30. Deep sea fishing $380-420 for six hours.

Sightseeing. Archaeological sites $1-5. Cozumel Museum $2. Xcaret Lagoon $10. Chankanaab Park $4. Xel-Há Lagoon $5.

Taxis. Plaza Caracol to downtown Cancún $5. Cancún to Playa del Carmen $27 (maximum four passengers).

POLICE (policía)

If have to deal with the police, for example if reporting a theft, and you do not speak fluent Spanish, then take along someone who does. The main police station in Cancún is downtown on Avenida Tulum, next to the State Tourism Office, with a smaller branch in the Hotel Zone near the Sheraton Hotel. See also CRIME AND THEFT, EMERGENCIES.

POST OFFICES (correo)

The main post office in **Cancún** is at the junction of Avenida Sunyaxchen and Avenida Xel-Há, open 8 a.m.-7 p.m. Monday-Friday, 9 a.m.-noon Saturday. In **Cozumel**, the post office is on Avenida Rafael E. Melgar, several blocks south of the Plaza, open 9 a.m.-1 p.m. and 3 p.m.-6 p.m. Monday-Friday, 9 a.m.-1 p.m. Saturday. Stamps (*estampillo*, *timbre*) can also be bought in newsagents and drugstores. Post boxes are blue and grey. Before posting anything, however, note that even airmail postcards and letters can take up to two weeks to reach the US and Canada, and can take even longer to get to Europe!

General delivery (*poste restante*). If you don't know in advance where you'll be staying, you can have your mail addressed a/c Lista de Correos, Cancún, Quintana Roo 77501, Mexico. Your surname should be in capital letters. When collecting mail, take along your **126** passport for identification.

I want to send a telegram to ...	**Quisiera mandar un telegrama a ...**	
Have you received any mail for...?	**¿Ha recibido correo para...?**	
stamp/letter/postcard	**timbre/carta/tarjeta**	
special delivery (express)	**urgente**	
airmail	**correo aéreo**	
registered	**registrado**	

PUBLIC HOLIDAYS (*dias festivos*)

Banks, government offices and many businesses are closed on the following dates.

1 January	*Año Nuevo*	New Year's Day
5 February	*Aniversario de la Constitución*	Constitution Day
21 March	*Nacimiento de Benito Juárez*	Benito Juárez's Birthday
1 May	*Dia del Trabajo*	Labor Day
5 May	*Batalla de Puebla*	Anniversary of the Battle of Puebla
1 September	*Informe presidencial*	First day of Congress
16 September	*Dia de la Independencia*	Independence Day
12 October	*Dia de la Raza*	Columbus Day, 'Day of the Race'
2 November	*Dia de los Muertos*	All Souls' Day
20 November	*Aniversario de la Revolucion*	Anniversary of the Revolution
12 December	*Nuestra Señora de Guadalupe*	Our Lady of Guadalupe
25 December	*Navidad*	Christmas Day
Movable dates *Pascua, Semana Santa*		Easter, Holy Week

Are you open tomorrow?	**¿Está abierto mañana?**

PUBLIC TRANSPORT

Ferries (*barco; transbordador*). Frequent passenger ferries run between Puerto Juárez (20 minutes by bus from downtown Cancún) and Isla Mujeres. There are several crossings daily, last boat back to Cancún leaves around 6.30 p.m. A less frequent (and more expensive) **127**

service departs from Playa Linda Marine Terminal in the Hotel Zone. Passenger ferries also operate between Playa del Carmen (42 miles (68 km) south of Cancún) and Cozumel. Both crossings take about 45 minutes.

Buses (*camion*). Cancún has a cheap and frequent bus service between downtown (*centro*) and the Hotel Zone (*Zona Hotelera*). Long-distance buses to Playa del Carmen, Tulum, and Meridá depart from the bus station at the junction of Avenidas Tulum and Uxmal. You will be more comfortable on the air-conditioned first class (*primera clase*) service.

R

RADIO and TELEVISION (*radio; televisión*)

Most hotels have satellite and cable television which broadcast American programmes and English-language movies. Short-wave radios will be able to pick up Voice of America, Radio Canada International and the BBC World Service. If you bring your own vehicle and have a citizen's band radio, there are three government-approved channels: one for communication between individual tourists, one for communication among a group of RVs (recreational vehicles) travelling as a caravan, and a third for contacting the Green Angels highway patrol (see also DRIVING).

RELIGIOUS SERVICES

Mexico is predominantly Roman Catholic. In Cancún, the Catholic Church of Cristo Rey is on Calle Margaritas, beside the Parque de Palapas. There is a Presbyterian church a few blocks away on Calle Crisantemos. Some of the luxury hotels hold services in English.

What time is mass/the service?	**¿A qué hora es la misa/el culto?**
Is it in English?	**¿Es en inglés?**

TAXIS *(taxi)*

There is no shortage of taxis in Cancún. The Hotel Zone throngs with the green and white city cabs, all honking hopefully at strolling tourists. You can hail one in the street, or have your hotel call one for you. Check with your hotel reception or the Tourism Office what the price for a particular journey ought to be, and always establish the fare with the driver before getting in. On Cozumel, a list of standard taxi fares is displayed at the entrance to the ferry pier. Taxis can also be hired for longer journeys, for example from Cancún to Playa del Carmen, or for a day's sightseeing. Again, negotiate and agree the price with the driver beforehand.

What's the fare to ...?	**¿Cuál es la tarifa a ...?**

TELEPHONES *(teléfonos)*

Look for the **Ladatel** phones which are now common in Cancún, Cozumel and Meridá. Some accept coins (100, 500, 1000 and 5000 pesos), some need a Ladatel Card (*una tarjeta Ladatel*), available from drugstores, while others accept credit cards. These phones are easy to use, and much cheaper than the hotel telephone. To make a local call, dial the number only. For long-distance calls within Mexico, dial 91 then area code followed by the number. For calls to the USA and Canada, dial 95, area code then number (for example, to call New York City, dial 95-212-number). For direct-dial calls to the rest of the world, dial 98, then country code, then area code (without the initial zero) then number (for example, to call central London, dial 98-44-71-number). For international calls it is much cheaper go through the English-speaking international operator (dial 09) and use your credit card, or ask for a collect call.

Can you get me this number?	**¿Puede comunicarme a este número?**
collect (reversed-charged) call	**por cobrar**
person-to-person (personal) call	**de persona a persona**

TIME DIFFERENCES

Yucatán is on US Central Standard Time, which is GMT minus six hours. There is no change to daylight saving time in summer.

New York	London	**Cancún**	Los Angeles	Chicago
1 p.m.	6 p.m.	**noon**	10 a.m.	noon

TIPPING

Wages are low in Cancún's tourist industry, and tips will make a significant contribution to local incomes. Reckon on 10-15% for waiters (unless a service charge has been included), the equivalent of 50 cents a bag for porters, $0.50-$1.00 a day for hotel maids and $1.00 for tour guides. It is not customary to tip taxi drivers.

Keep the change.   **Déjelo para usted.**

TOILETS (*baños; sanitarios*)

There are well maintained public toilets in shopping malls and at archaeological sites and other tourist attractions. The men's toilet will be labelled *caballeros* or H (for *hombres*), the women's *damas* or M (for *mujeres*). If there is an attendant, a small tip is expected.

Where are the toilets?   **¿Dónde están los sanitarios?**

TOURIST INFORMATION OFFICES (*oficina de turismo*)

For information before you leave home, contact one of the following Mexican Government Tourism Offices.

In Canada:
2 Bloor Street West, Suite 1801,
Toronto, Ontario M4W 3E2.
  Tel. 416 925 0704.

In the UK:
60-61 Trafalgar Square,
London WC2N 5DS.
  Tel. 071 734 1058.

In the USA:
405 Park Avenue, Suite 1002,
New York, NY 10022.
  Tel. 212 755 7212.

Once in Mexico you can get information and assistance from the Federal Tourism Office (Secretaría de Turismo, SECTUR), at the corner of Avenida Cobá and Avenida Nader in downtown Cancún, tel. 988 843238, or one of the following Tourism Offices:

Avenida Tulum 26, Cancún;
  Tel. 988 848073.

2nd floor, Plaza del Sol,
Avenida Benito Juárez, Cozumel;
  Tel. 987 21915.

Teatro Péon Contreras,
Calle 60 (between Calles 57 and 59), Mérida;
  Tel. 99 249290.

An independent tourist information agency called Cancún Tips has a booth in the Plaza Caracol in the Hotel Zone. They publish a handy booklet containing maps, lists of shops and restaurants, and other useful information.

WATER (*agua*)

Most hotels and restaurants automatically provide purified water (*agua purificada*). Never drink water from the tap. Bottled Mexican mineral water, naturally carbonated, is pure and delicious. Bottled or canned soft drinks and juices are always safe to drink. See also MEDICAL CARE on p.121.

a bottle of mineral water	**una botella de agua mineral**
carbonated/non-carbonated	**con gas/sin gas**

YOUTH HOSTELS *(albergue de la juventud)*

CREA (Consejo Nacional de Recursos para la Atencionde la Juventud) runs a Youth Hostel in Cancún, situated at the north end of the Hotel Zone, only a mile and a half (2 km) from downtown, with its own beach. Beds in single-sex dormitories are available to holders of International Youth Hostels Federation cards. For more information on youth hostelling in Mexico, contact the Agencia Nacional de Turismo Juvenil, Glorieta del Metro Insurgentes, Local CC-11, Col. Juárez, CP06600 Mexico DF.

NUMBERS

0	**cero**	17	**diecisiete**
1	**uno**	18	**dieciocho**
2	**dos**	19	**diecinueve**
3	**tres**	20	**veinte**
4	**cuatro**	21	**veintiuno**
5	**cinco**	40	**cuarenta**
6	**seis**	50	**cincuenta**
7	**siete**	60	**sesenta**
8	**ocho**	70	**setenta**
9	**nueve**	80	**ochenta**
10	**diez**	90	**noventa**
11	**once**	100	**cien**
12	**doce**	101	**ciento uno**
13	**trece**	102	**ciento dos**
14	**catorce**	500	**quinientos**
15	**quince**	1,000	**mil**
16	**dieciséis**		

DAYS OF THE WEEK

Sunday	**domingo**
Monday	**lunes**
Tuesday	**martes**
Wednesday	**miércoles**
Thursday	**jueves**
Friday	**viernes**
Saturday	**sábado**

Index

Page numbers in italic refer to photographs.